SUNYATA

The Life & Sayings
of a
Rare-born
Mystic

edited and compiled
by
Betty Camhi
and
Elliott Isenberg

North Atlantic Books
Berkeley, California

SUNYATA
The Life & Sayings of a Rare-born Mystic

Copyright © 1990 by Betty Camhi and Elliott Isenberg
ISBN 1-55643-096-5
All rights reserved

Second edition, 1993

Publisher's address:
North Atlantic Books
P.O. Box 12327
Berkeley, California 94701

Editors' mailing address:
Betty Camhi,
5123 W. Griffin Creek Road,
Medford, Oregon 97501-9637

Cover and book design by Paula Morrison
Typeset by Campaigne & Associates Typography
Printed in the United States of America

SUNYATA: The Life & Sayings of a Rare-born Mystic is sponsored by the Society for the Study of Native Arts and Sciences, a nonprofit educational corporation whose goals are to develop an ecological and crosscultural perspective linking various scientific, social, and artistic fields; to nurture a holistic view of arts, sciences, humanities, and healing; and to publish and distribute literature on the relationship of mind, body, and nature.

Library of Congress Cataloging-in-Publication Data
Sunyata, 1890–1984.
    Sunyata : the life & sayings of a rare-born mystic / edited by
Betty Camhi, Elliott Isenberg.
        p.   cm.
    Includes biographical references.
    ISBN 1-55643-096-5 : $12.95
    1. Sunyata, 1890–1984.   2. Mystics—Biography.   I. Camhi, Betty
II. Isenberg, Elliott.   III. Title.
BL625.S82A3 1990
294.5' 092—dc20   90-46597
    [B]   CIP

The man of Tao
remains unknown;
Perfect virtue
produces nothing;
'No-Self' is
'true-Self';
And the greatest man
is Nobody.

—Chuang Tzu
xvii. 3.
(composed in the 4th century B.C.)

I'm Nobody! Who are you?
Are you—Nobody—too?
Then there's a pair of us!

—Emily Dickinson
Poem 288
(composed in 1861)

Dedicated
to
spiritual seekers
everywhere

CONTENTS

Who Was Sunyata?

We have attempted to piece together some of Sunyata's life, mostly from recalled answers in the weekly gatherings over the years that we knew him. As Sunyata was of "no mind," his own stories never fit into any neat chronological order.

(Any words that have been *italicized* can be found in the **Glossary** at the end of the book.)

Sunyata was born on a small Danish farm in 1890 with the name of Alfred Julius Emmanuel Sorensen. At the time of his birth, his two sisters were 12 and 14 years old. As he was only educated up to the 8th grade, he would often joke that he had escaped "**head**ucation." During his childhood, a big shock occurred when he was 14 and the family farm was sold to strangers who had no respect for the land. He began an apprenticeship in horticulture, and eventually moved to England where he became "a simple gardener."

As a gardener, he worked from 6 in the morning to 6 in the evening in such big estates as Forty Hall, Sunbury Court, Hampton Court, and Dartington Hall. While he was working on the gardens of Dartington Hall in Devonshire, Rabindranath Tagore, the Indian poet, came to speak. Emmanuel (this means the "indwelling God" and was Sunya's favorite Western name for himself) played a Beethoven quartet for Tagore on an old gramophone; Tagore was so impressed with the quality of Emmanuel's silence (lack of willfulness and ego desires) that he invited him "to come to India to teach silence." But how can you teach something except by being It? Being It he was, and his arrival in India in 1930—in his 40th year—marked the beginning of a new phase in his life's drama. People immediately thrust titles upon him like 'baba', 'saint', and 'guru', but none of these names seemed true to his being. He did accept small gifts from people, but refused them if they were more than he needed at the time. For 48 years he was to live in India, where his work was simply to BE and his days as a gardener a thing of the past. Everything was given to him. In Sunyata's words: "We live so close to Heaven."

In order to better grasp the next chapter of this story, it is necessary to know something about Ramana Maharshi (1879–1950), the sage of Arunachala, who was made famous in the West by Paul Brunton's book *A Search in Secret India*. Ramana had realized the Self at the age of 16, and lived the rest of his life near the sacred hill named Arunachala. Paul Brunton had visited Ramana in the early 1930's and was struck by the power of his Silence. Although Emmanuel first heard of Ramana Maharshi from an American whom he met in Kashmir, he subsequently read Paul Brunton's book, and decided to make the pilgrimage to visit Ramana.

Once he arrived there in 1936, Emmanuel soon realized that he had never before met this quality of consciousness in any living being. Later in his life, he said about this meeting:

Never before had I awared such integral Self-Radiance in any human form, such light of Silence. One was being fed just awaring him. At the first sight of him, I felt no excitement or even awe, no solemnity or ecstasy, simply a calm recognition, a glad contentment, and gratitude in his *darshan*.

When Emmanuel first arrived, Ramana asked him his name and nationality, and inquired about mutual friends and his *sadhana* (the Way he had come). Emmanuel was put up in one of the ashram guest houses and during his two week stay spent many of his days sitting in the back of the meditation hall soaking in the quality of Ramana's radiance. Unlike most of the other Westerners who came to visit the ashram, Emmanuel did not ask even one question; other than his response to those few initial questions from Ramana, there was no verbal communication between them. Emmanuel was therefore quite surprised when he later heard from Paul Brunton that (soon after his departure) Ramana had referred to him as a *janam-siddha*— "one of the rare-born mystics." When Emmanuel heard this phrase "rare-born mystic," he had no idea of what a "mystic" was or what it meant to be one who was "rare-born." Emmanuel soon acquired a copy of *The Oxford Book of English Mystical Verse* in the hope of finding out what it meant to be a "mystic." At the same time he began to examine his own childhood to see why he had been able to so easily loosen his identification with ego-consciousness; it was this exploration that was the origin of the reflections called **Memory.**

It was during Emmanuel's third visit to Ramana Maharshi in 1940 that he acquired the name that he was to use for the rest of his life. He was just sitting quietly in meditation when he awared an effulgence—a spiritual flood of light—especially radiated and directed upon his form and suddenly out of the

Silence came an (unsolicited) telepathic message from Ramana
Maharshi in the form of these five English words:

We are always aware sunyata.

What surprised him most in this message was the word
"always"—although he had often transmuted Shakespeare's
phrase that "ripeness is all" into his own saying "awareness
is all," up to that moment he had never realized that who he
was is **always** "aware." He also asked himself who is this
"we"? Did it mean Ramana Maharshi and himself or did it
include everyone? Eventually he concluded that "we" is the
indwelling, *innerstanding* Word, Logos, Sophia—the androgynous EmmanuEL. Another surprise was that Ramana, a
Hindu sage, had used the Buddhist term *"sunyata"*, a term often
translated as "the void" or "full solid emptiness". The Buddhist
doctrine of *sunyata* asserts that all beings and phenomena are
free of any soul or intrinsic nature; this means that although
people, things, and events appear on the outside to be real and
substantial, they are actually—when innerstood—ephemer-
al and insubstantial. Sunyata took Ramana's five words as
recognition, initiation, mantra, and name. Thereafter, he referred
to both himself and the hut in which he lived as "Sunyata".
Like a crystal that reflects many colors yet itself remains pure,
clear, unaffected, that's who he would always be, no-thing-
ness. *Tat twam asi,* he was fond of saying—**"Thou art That"**.

For the next four decades, Sunyata continued to live in his
Himalayan hut not far from Almora. About his new home,
so beautifully situated with vast views of a vaster Silence, he
said, "I was contented in Denmark though I could see the oth-

ers regarded me as an oddity. In England I felt freer. In India I felt at home. But in the Himalayas I feel closest to Heaven." During all these years in India, he was never employed, but found money being pushed on him. He was once offered 20 rupees a month ($2.50), but only accepted 5. Then in 1950, the Birla Foundation in New Delhi (whose purpose is to assist saints and saddhus) asked him if he'd accept 100 rupees a month and he agreed to accept 20. "It was more than I needed at the time," he admitted, "but I thought prices might rise." It was later raised to 50 rupees where it remained for more than 20 years. Even after inflation made it hard to live on 50, Sunyata would never consider getting a raise through asking.

Living nearby to his Himalayan hut on "Crank's Ridge" were such neighbors as the Tibetan Buddhist scholars Lama Anagarika Govinda and Dr. Walter Y. Evans-Wentz. He would often make pilgrimages to the plains of India during the winter season, and return to his hut—high in the mountains—when the plains began to sizzle with the summer heat. He became personally acquainted with such leaders of the Indian independence movement as Mahatma Gandhi and Jawaharlal Nehru. He also came to know Anandamayi Ma and Neem Karoli Baba and many realized beings who are virtually unknown in the West.

The story of Sunyata's stay in India would not be complete without mentioning his plucky small black-and-white dog named "Wuti". Wuti was brought from Tibet in a sack along with a lion cub in 1950, and he became Sunyata's constant companion for the next 9 years. Sunyata named him Wuti because that was the sound he made when he barked. An Indian saint named Anandamayi Ma looked at Wuti and announced, "This is not a dog." Thereafter, she permitted Wuti into the inner sanctum of her ashram where no dogs were allowed. After Wuti died, Sunyata changed Wuti's name to Wuji and used this term—Wuji—to refer to his own higher Self. When Sunyata was asked why he changed his name from Wuti to Wuji, he replied: "Adding 'ji' to a name is what is done in India to show respect—the dog needed less bark and more bite."

Sunyata would have been happy and content to live in India for the remainder of his bodily-life. He never had any desire to go anywhere, let alone to America. In November 1973, a group of seekers from California associated with the Alan Watts Society went to India to visit Lama Govinda, Sunyata's friend and neighbor. A local villager just happened to mention to this group that there lived a solitary hermit-type-ancient-one whom they might want to visit. They went to Sunyata's hut and decided that he indeed was an Enlightened One. One of the group members told him "You'll be in California next year." Sunyata protested: "But I have nothing to teach and nothing to sell." The gentleman replied: "That's why we want you!"—and off he trotted. Eventually, one of these visitors sent Sunyata a round-trip plane ticket to California with the promise: "Reality-wise, Sunyata need not do anything."

When he was invited to settle in America, Sunyata believed that his life was drawing to an end; here he was a man in his 80's who had spent many of the last decades in silence. Over the years, however, he had developed a language to talk about his Reality and had discovered that there was an unusually good rapport with some of the spiritual seekers who had come from the West to visit India. *"Prarabdha karma,"* Sunyata once explained, "is the karma that cannot be changed in one's lifetime." So it was his *prarabdha karma* to first come to America at the tender young age of 84. One of the few places in America that had ever really interested him was — coincidentally — California. When he was a young man living in England, he had been exposed to the teachings of Theosophists who had spoken about a New Race of people being born in several geographical locations, one of which was supposed to be in California. If a New Race was being born, he wanted to be there for the birthing.

So for the last six years of his life, he made his home in California. "I take my home with me wherever I go," he said. He made no effort "to do" anything—his mode was simply "to be". Many people claimed that significant changes in their life would occur after meeting him. "I do nothing, it just happens," he would always say.

"Every thing always happens rightly," he would say to his fellow pilgrims, "all is right that seems most wrong."

While crossing a busy intersection in Fairfax, California on the morning of Sunday, August 5th, 1984, he was struck by a car. He was taken to nearby Ross Hospital, but by that evening he had entered into a coma. He lived another eight days, but never regained consciousness.

Betty's Recollections

In 1978, I moved to Marin County—just across the Golden Gate Bridge from San Francisco. I telephoned a good friend and asked him what folks here in Marin did in the evenings. He replied, "They go to the Sunyata gatherings." I told my friend that I was tired of chasing after gurus as I had been doing that for the last few years of my life; but my friend assured me that this man was different. So one Thursday evening, aboard the old Alan Watts houseboat, I found myself listening to the voice of an elderly man, dressed in Indian clothes and turban, who spoke with a soft Danish accent. I had previously met teachers whom you could rarely get near because there were so many people who wanted to be with them. Sunyata made no claims about being anyone in particular and he was very easy to approach and to talk to. I was charmed by his utter simplicity and seeming ordinariness. In the days, months, and years to follow, Sunya-Bhai was to become my dearest, most cherished Friend.

When the Alan Watts Society "kidnapped" this fellow Sunyata from his Himalayan sanctuary, they did so with the conviction that the arrival of a genuinely Enlightened One would bring crowds so numerous that they would have to be turned away. This, much to my relief, never happened. I think this was due to his lack of "flash"—he had no interest in power, fame, or money; he didn't do healings, wasn't psychic and performed no miracles. For those seekers who wanted a teacher to be "spectacular," it was anti-climactic to hear him continually insist that he was a "no-body" and that since he had attained "no-thing," he had "nothing to teach and nothing to sell."

In India, he was revered by many as a saint. Since the Silence of his Being radiated, he was given the highest regard in a country that doesn't easily accept non-Indians as one of their own. Here in America, where simplicity is rarely viewed as a virtue, only a handful of people appreciated—or even apperceived—this "rare-born mystic."

Rabindranath Tagore, in his first meeting with Emmanuel, awared a Silence so profound that he invited Emmanuel to "come to India to teach silence." This silence was a complete lack of the usual desires that most of us take for normal; there was no desire for his life to be any different from the way it was. At the time Tagore met Emmanuel he was working long days as a gardener earning minimal wages. Most people would dream about getting out of such circumstances and of improving their lot in life, but such was not the case with Emmanuel. He accepted everything that happened to him and he was simply at ease in all of life's circumstances. He was like the chameleon that could adapt and fit into situations that were as various and varied as the continents and countries he lived in.

Paradoxically, even if he excelled at adapting to his surroundings, there was a sameness about him, something that never changed, regardless of where he was or who he was with. I once heard a tape recording of Sunyata talking to that first group of Western seekers who had burst into his Himalayan sanctuary in 1973. His words and demeanor were exactly the same as when I met him five years later in California. He was *samata*, the unchanging awareness amidst changing forms. "Aware that which does not change in all that changes," he would advise, "*Tat twam asi*—thou art That."

During most of his life Sunyata was a quiet listener and did not seek to impose, share, or even to discuss his consciousness with others. Growing up in Denmark, he was not really understood by his own family and his mother once commented that she thought him "a bit queer." Her opinion, as well as the opinions of others, did not concern him. When he accepted Tagore's invitation to visit India and people thrust such names upon him as baba, guru, and saint, he remained unaffected. Sunyata would often say: "What Peter says about Paul says more about Peter than Paul. Do not dissipate your energy trying to explain yourself to others. Simply radiate your light."

In India people who regarded Sunyata as a guru sought his blessing and tried to thrust things upon him; however he would never accept more than what he needed. The "curse" of possessions and property was never anything he desired. The only thing he readily accepted was books—which he always shared. When he read the collection of recorded talks given by Nisargadatta Maharaj entitled *I Am That*, he was so impressed with the quality of consciousness in this book that he obtained as many copies as he could in order to give them away. He was indeed very generous with the small amount of money people gave to him.

Sunyata taught by being what he was and by the radiance of his light. From time to time there would appear at his home or at the weekly *satsangs*, people who were somewhat unbalanced, "troublemakers" as we came to call them. Sunyata did not make their appearance an issue. He never reacted to these people or gave them the attention needed to sustain their mischief; they would eventually disappear from the gatherings, leaving him once again at peace.

Sunyata never prayed for anyone or anything. "Why pray?" he would say. "Things are so beautifully right as they are. God's will is always being done, whether we like it or not. Things that seem to be wrong or going badly are really right and correct when viewed from the Whole, from the larger perspective. It is to egos that things seem to be wrong. 'There's a divinity that shapes our ends, rough-hew them though we may.' There is no real choice in life; all that we can do is to change our attitude towards what happens and that makes all the difference. Acceptance of all, the shadow and the light, is the key to living."

He radiated a joy, a peace, and an energy that he was unaware of. When people would comment to him about this wonderful energy that seemed to radiate from him, he would say, "I do not know what I do. We are constantly being used by the invisible forces and we are simply the actors on the stage of life. We think we push and pull and control events, but all the while we are being pushed and pulled and used. Do not complain or cry or pray, but open your intuitive eye and aware the light in and around you; it is forever."

Sunyata lived a life that was filled with Grace, ease, love, and wisdom. This was his teaching, his legacy. He was a mature "baby"—living in that non-dual state that babes are born into, but all too quickly fall out of. He had the non-dualistic glow of the new-born combined with the ripeness that manifests only after a long lifetime of living. He was very fond of saying, "Seek ye first the inner realm of Grace and all (mere) things shall be added unto you." He would remind us to consciously aim at this grace awareness. He emphasized that this was the most important thing in life, our most important pursuit, our highest attainment. Mere things are unimportant compared to this Grace, this living of "Heaven on Earth."

How was our time spent together? I offered to be his chauffeur, and our favorite pastime was visiting various friends. His neighbors from near Almora—Lama Govinda and Li Gotami—were now living just a few miles down the road in Mill Valley, and we would often drop in for tea and news about mutual friends. Sunyata was invited to speak in homes, in bookstores, in lecture-halls, and in churches. He was also very fond of coffee shops and I spent many hours with him drinking up his wisdom along with the coffee.

Sunyata would often say, "I never sought guru or guidance. When in my life, minor problems arose, I always went within for the answer. I never reached out to others for what I should or should not do." Whenever I would express some concern about my own personal future, he would say, "Step by step as thou goeth, the way shall open up to thee."

Friday evenings were a particularly special time for me. As it was the end of a week of teaching school, I would look forward to a few days of rest. My usual routine was to do grocery shopping and then to return home to cook dinner. While preparing food, sometime in the early evening, there would be this gentle knock at my door and it would be Sunyata. The proximity of my house to the post office made it easy for him to stop by in order to give me some of the writing that he wanted typed. He would stay for dinner and we would talk for hours. Then, because it was too dark for him to walk back alone, I would drive him home. Although this same scene repeated itself every Friday evening for as long as he lived in Mill Valley, each week it came as a delightful surprise.

Sunyata had always promised everyone that he would be around for his 100th birthday celebration . . . "unless," he would sometimes add, "I wind up in a hospital."

Events arrange themselves to carry out the Grand Plan; somewhere, I suppose, it was written that this Ancient One was to be crossing the street at the precise location where the car that struck him was to pass . . . and that he was to enter a hospital for the only time in his long and blessed life. His *prarabdha karma* had fulfilled itself and so his physical heart and breath stopped playing in the external Self-interplay.

Life is mysterious, a mystery to be lived and it is everlasting. I am grateful to the Blessed One who brought me closer to mySelf, and taught me what I did not know, that I-You-We are all Divine. In India, they have no word for thank you. How can you thank yourSelf for your Self?

Blessings to Wuji, Brother Emmanuel, Sunya-Bhai, and the Reader who happens upon this book.

Elliott's Recollections

I met Sunyata for the first time in the summer of 1981. A friend had told me about a 90-year old "mystic" who was holding a question-and-answer period once a week on a houseboat that had been owned by the philosopher Alan Watts. I thought it would be fun to meet a "mystic," so I agreed to go with my friend the very next week.

When I arrived at the evening gathering, Sunyata hadn't yet entered the central room of the houseboat, so I just sat upon a cushion and waited patiently for his arrival. Then I saw an unusually dressed person enter from the back of the room and nimbly make a pathway through the people sitting upon the floor. His appearance was both striking and other-worldly; he wore loose-fitting Indian-style pants and shirt, and around his head was wrapped a large turban; all of his clothing was of the same hue of light purple. He sat upon a chair facing those who had gathered that evening, and began the meeting with a few minutes of silence. Then, speaking softly with his ever so slight Danish accent, he told about his life and how he had been "kidnapped" and taken to America; he concluded this 5-minute introduction by saying that he had "nothing to teach and nothing to sell." He then asked if there were any questions. As he answered the questions, he would often smile and make jokes, and he always seemed to be radiating gentleness and playfulness. He was quite relaxed and exuded an air of confidence. I saw that neither by listening to his voice nor by looking at his face would I have been able to tell whether Sunyata was a man or a woman. At that first meeting, I realized that Sunyata possessed a rare humility and that he had told the truth when he had said he had "nothing to teach and nothing to sell."

I became a regular visitor at these weekly gatherings. At that time I had just started doing research for my doctoral dissertation; because of the sustained mental concentration needed for the research, I often found myself a bundle of nerves. It was only when I was in Sunyata's presence that I was able to contact a silent part of myself. In my week away from Sunyata, I would accumulate quite a bit of anxiety and tension, and then during my weekly visits I would watch as my nervous energy dissolved and melted away. Sunyata would often say that his life had been worry-free. When asked how this was possible, he would answer that in order to feel worry, it was necessary to be in your "head" and—he would playfully exclaim—"I've never been **head**ucated." And I would think, "Here I am in the final stages of my **head**ucation—and it seems all I do is worry."

What was undeniable to me was that Sunyata was having a different experience of life than anyone else I had ever known. I could sense his spontaneous and natural ease in accepting—and even embracing—opposites that seemed to me to be irreconcilable. He was always playful, and I never noticed in him even a trace of sadness or resentment. Over a period of several years, I saw how anyone who spent any time with him would comment how they had never met a person who radiated so much peace.

When in his presence, I could see how it was my desires,

fears, and expectations that were cutting me off from the Silence that was always there. Sunyata was like an ocean-bound river that was always murmuring cheerfully no matter what the appearance of the scenery that was passing by; just to sit by that river gave me a calm sense of detachment and inward peace.

At one of these gatherings, Sunyata made the prophecy that the word *innerstand* — a word that he himSelf had invented—would one day be in the dictionary. When asked what he meant by *innerstand,* he said:

> Here in the West, people are so mental—
> they **understand** rather than **innerstand**.

After hearing him use the word *innerstand* in a variety of contexts, I gathered that it was a way of comprehending that was not mental. Because it came directly from the beyond, it required no words, thought, or even effort—but only intuitive apperception. According to Sunyata, only when one became mind-free—not necessarily free **of** mind, but certainly free **in** mind—could one begin to *innerstand.* Sunyata believed that as Westerners became more trusting of their intuition that they would feel a need to find new words that honored this sense, and he offered the words *innerstand* and *innerstanding* as his gifts to the English language.

Two years after meeting Sunyata, I finally did receive my doctoral degree; it was a special treat for me to have Sunyata come to my graduation as my guest of honor. He sat right next to me, and I felt blessed to have such a friend.

And I did experience Sunyata as a friend. He made himself so accessible—I could call him on the telephone and have a chat, or even arrange a visit to his house. Because he was so un-imposing, I found myself drawing closer and closer to him. Occasionally I would experience him as my "brother," but then I would remember how old he was, and he would suddenly become my wise old "grandfather." But most of all, he was a friend.

Like most of the people around him, I assumed he would be around for his 100th birthday. In all his 93 years, he had never been sick or even had such a minor ailment as a headache. He had never seen the inside of a hospital. I just figured that since he was stress-free, he was aging at an extremely slow pace. He would often joke about how he would invite the Queen of Denmark to his 100th birthday party, and—even if he claimed that he had no psychic powers—I just assumed that he knew that the event would happen with him there in his bodily form.

When I learned he was hit by a car, I came quickly to visit the hospital. Within the first moment of the visit, I awared that he was never going to recover. He was (barely) in his body, hanging onto it by merely a thread. But—to my amazement—I could feel Sunyata's "awareness" permeating the entire room. On some non-verbal level that had never been possible before, I innerstood that who Sunyata is was not his body and that who he is is "**always** aware."

During the year following Sunyata's death, I had many vivid dreams with him as the main character. Exactly one year after that day by his bedside in the hospital, I had this dream:

I am with Sunyata, and from the beginning I feel this is a "special" visit, but yet Sunyata is making no fuss or hoopla. As those surrounding Sunyata and myself realize that

Sunyata has come for a visit from the land of the dead, they become agitated and upset trying to figure out how to best honor him on this "special" occasion. But, amidst this growing bustle and commotion, Sunyata just remains calm and placid; it is as if he is telling us that even during a visit that seems so "special," he needs no "special" honor as he is never impressed by his own "specialness" or the "specialness" of any occasion.

I do feel that I was visited by Sunyata; it certainly seemed natural that since he never thought of himself as "special" when he was in bodily form, he would not have considered it "special" to have made a visit from the land of the dead.

I would like to take this opportunity to express my appreciation for this friend who came from the land of Wuji. The final irony for me is that a mystic who had "nothing to teach" was the one who "taught" me that Silence is the gateway to the Real.

Editors' Note

Sunyata: The Life & Sayings of a Rare-born Mystic has two main parts, the first main part—on the pages to the right—is called **Memory**. Sunyata is using the term "memory" in the same sense that Socrates used the term *anamnesis*—usually translated as "recollection"— to refer to the remembrance of a wisdom that is possessed before birth, but lost at the moment of birth. In these reflections, Sunyata is exploring how it happened that he never totally lost touch with this pre-natal awareness of wholeness, unity, and living harmonies. Sunyata tells his life story—of how he only briefly identified with his ego-consciousness—and describes what it feels like to be in such a state of ego-free consciousness. **Memory** was written in Sunyata's Himalayan hermitage during 1945; however, when Sunyata discovered in 1980 that the first few pages of **Memory** had been destroyed, he wrote a new beginning to the story.

The second main part of this book—on the pages to the left—includes many of Sunyata's favorite sayings, some of which were repeated over and over again to fellow pilgrims. As often as we could, we have included the name of the original author who inspired these sayings. As will be noted, Sunyata would often purposely change some of the wording in a famous quotation to make the saying more in tune with his own innerstanding; we have indicated that the quotation is not an exact duplication of the original by writing "with respects to" and then giving the name of the original author.

Changes have been made in **Memory** to improve the grammar, spelling, and comprehensibility. The story of Sunyata's life, the notes, the fairytale, the bibliography, the chronology, and the glossary have been added by us.

Marianne Thorborg Jensen, a Danish friend of the editors, made a new translation of Sunyata's favorite Hans Christian Andersen fairytale so as to bring forth the religious luster of the original tale that had been lost in many of the earlier translations.

We want to thank Peder Baek, the great grandchild of Sunyata's sister, for obtaining the family's permission to publish **Memory**. Once we received this permission, we were given a renewed faith that now was the moment to bring Sunyata's writings to the attention of a wider audience.

It is with gratitude to Wuji that we leave you with the words of one born Emmanuel Sorensen.

> Betty Camhi
> Elliott Isenberg
> 8 March 1990

MEMORY

They shall call his name Emmanuel
(which means, God with us).

—*Matthew* 1:23

All inquiry and all learning
is
but recollection.

—Socrates
Plato's *Meno* 81

A great man is one
who never loses
the heart of a new-born babe.
The sole concern of learning
is to seek
one's original heart.

—Mencius
Book IV, Part B, 12
Book VI, Part A, 11

These retrospective musings, on pre-ego and pre-natal memory bubbled up in 1945 in a Himalayan hermitage. It wanted to be and so emerged, writing itSelf through us. Some copies were sent to friends, who all were aware that the terms Emmanuel, Wuji, and I, pertained to one and the same persona-mask or individual uniqueness in the Individuum. Now, 35 years later, a friend has taken the trouble to type it and so made it readable for *egojies*. Unfortunately, some pages were missing at the very beginning of the manuscript and so, Sri Emmanuel, who is now commonly known as "Sunyata," 90 years young and dwelling in California, has been asked by himSelf to remember and rewrite a beginning to this beginningless *memory*.

Emmanuel Sorensen took body and birth, this time, in Denmark, the year was 1890, on a small and rather isolated farm. He had a very quiet and solitary childhood that was harmoniously and congenially related to both nature and to his fellow humans. It was so simple and unconditioned that the first 7 years are remembered as pre-ego consciousness. Ego and mind were no trouble, as there were no impositions, no training, no discipline, and no sin-complex. But there was consciousness and even a certain unconscious awareness of wholeness, unity, and living harmonies, which he later on came to call *memory*. Socrates had used this same term—*memory*—to refer to the recollection of a light of awareness possessed before birth.[1] Similarly, Mencius, the Chinese sage who lived a century after Socrates, saw the purpose of education as remembering one's "original heart". Wise it is not to dissipate and blur this *memory* in word-symbols or by trying to

Innerstand.
It will be a new word in the dictionary.
There are innerstances and circumstances.
Innerstanding is intuitive awareness—
it is not mental at all.

To "understand" intellectually—
which means to "stand under,"
in other words,
to be burdened by mental conceptions—
prevents one from grasping the Truth.

—Anandamayi Ma
Words of Sri Anandamayi Ma,
Chapter 17

tell, express, or explain It to others. When one innerstands, there is never any craving to prove or assert, or any fluttering to gain understanding or love.

At seven years of body age, school and *egojies* happened upon Emmanuel—and, in duality play, he felt at first a breach, or a loss of some thing real, but only for a brief while. Soon also duality and ego-fuss were accepted in joyous ease. Ego-consciousness and pre-ego-consciousness could be co-existing and unclashing, and still are, although now they are sometimes overshadowed by post-ego consciousness. *Wu!*

In 1904, our farm was sold to strangers. Until then, there was still harmonious solitude on the farm. *Beate Solitude. Sole Beatitude*[2]—it was this beatitude of the first 14 years of Emmanuel's life span which established the rhythm for a life harmonious with *memory*. This simple, peasant lad escaped what he calls *headucation*—mental conditioning, impositions, ambition, and the "curse" of desiring property. *Headucation* never happened to come upon him and he neither craved nor reached out for it. He also had no need for external guru-guidance, a father-confessor, or even for intimate friends in whom he could confide. From the beginning, he *innerstood*: "The Source and I are One."

There were 4 years of apprenticeship in agriculture in Denmark, and then in 1911, he went to England. For 19 years, Emmanuel lived in England, earning his livelihood as a simple gardener—frugally and with poor, but sufficient wages—all in glad contentment and joyous ease, happy and harm-free, aye in conscious and unconscious grace awareness.

At Dartington Hall in Devonshire, the Indian poet Rabindranath Tagore befriended the simple gardener and sug-

"Know" and "understand" are too mental—says *Wuji*.
He'd rather use "sense," "aware," "intuit," and
"innerstand."
He seems to *innerstand* the Ghostly Whole.

Written to our Self,
the naughty word-symbols "I," "me," and "mine"
do not occur—
we *innerstand*.

Self-controlled spontaneity
is not a matter of **under**-standing or *over*-standing,
or of knowing,
achieving,
conquering,
or controlling
something or anything—
but, rather, of *inner-standing*,
in empathy and integral awareness here and now.

Where nothing is said, all may be innerstood.

gested that he "come to India to teach Silence." This casual invitation brought Emmanuel to Bharat in 1930 and there he lived happily—at joyous ease—for the next 48 years. His main residence was a Himalayan cave-like hut, but he would visit friends in the plains during the cool seasons. He was befriended by Bapuji Gandhi and the Jawaharlal Nehru family[3] by Anandamayi Ma, and by saints and sages galore, Maha-atmas and Self-realized fellow pilgrims in Eternity.

Ramana Maharshi discerned in Emmanuel "one of the rare-born mystics"—and gave his initiation with these words: "We are always aware sunyata." In 1973, Yankee guys and girlies invaded the Himalayan Turiya Sanctuary and one of them peremptorily shouted, "You shall be in California next year!" Emmanuel protested, "But we[4] have nothing to teach and nothing to sell"—and he was told, "That is why we want you."

So it happened in due time, according to our *prarabdha karma*, we let our Self be kidnapped to the far West by the almost almighty Bhagwan Sri Dollar, whom we fortunately can happily ignore, still at joyous ease in *Swa-lila*, happy and harmfree, aye more than merely happy—*anandaful* in Grace awareness. *Wu!*[5]

On the solitary farm in Denmark were tree friends, animals, birds, and humans—all in harmonious Self-interplay and interdependence. My father was a farmer and the son of a farmer; he was competent but very quiet, unassuming, and

In silence you can accept.
Silence and solitude was my speciality from childhood.
I did not reach out for other people.
I accepted them when they came,
but I did not reach out,
not even for knowledge or ambition,
nor to become anything, no.
And that was my wisdom from childhood,
a kind of natural maturity.

When one lives harmoniously and masticates well,
one needs very little food—
whenever possible,
eat slowly, religiously, silently, and alone.

I was never mental.
The mind did not develop—
I never had to go to school.
The mind is so troublesome here in the West—
you're so mental.
In India, there is intuitive awareness—
they're not mental in your sense of the word.
The mind-ridden ego,
the ego-ridden mind,
they're very much the same.

almost ego-free—living in simple contentment, uncraving, unassertive, unaggressive, and harmoniously at Home in the graceful Life-play. Mother was the same, but more talkative and more social. There were two sisters 12 and 14 years older than their baby brother; Jeusine worked as a Red Cross nurse and Mary married in 1897; there was no apparent influence from them and very few common memories. Servants and helpers were hired at harvest time, and all lived in harmony, naturalness, and joyous ease.

Emmanuel accepted what happened—even enjoyed and endured it—and had no need or urge to seek the company of others. Usually Emmanuel was a quiet listener, spectator, and observer, in almost unconscious empathy with visitors and people he met or visited. He listened and was interested in fellow wayfarers and in happenings around him. He especially enjoyed biographies, mystic poetry, and such novelists as Fyodor Dostoyevsky, Leo Tolstoy, D. H. Lawrence, Aldous Huxley, and the plays by Henrik Ibsen, Anton Chekhov, and William Shakespeare.

As a child he vibrated vicariously with the desire-rhythms of talkers. Most talkers, when they get an intelligent enough listener or a quiet sympathetic audience, enjoy themselves and go on and on; to listen patiently was both a discipline and a power. He learned their various languages though he could not speak them. He also found them interesting up to a point. The ability to listen and respond passively developed a flexibility and an awareness of the beautiful differences among *egojies*. He had his own rhythm and rightness in Silence, and with this as a background, he listened and responded patiently, contentedly, and unassertively. But at other times, it became

A woman Sufi friend living in India said of Sunyata:
"When he enters the room,
he does it so quietly and unobtrusively
that one hardly notices him.
He is responsive to questions and to the circumstances,
but he makes no speeches, no assertions,
and very few statements—
yet, when he leaves,
the room is suddenly felt to be empty."

I am not interested in what men can say with words—
I am interested only in what they can say with their Silence.
You must realize that men who talk well, and who utter
beautiful speeches, usually have a very bad Silence.
What is really important is Silence, for it is a preparation for
the **Great Silence**.

—Sunyata's telepathic communication to Miguel Serrano—
as recorded in Serrano's
The Serpent of Paradise:
The Story of an Indian Pilgrimage,
Chapter 33.

tiresome to listen; to hear the same Jazz-tune again and again and again may weary a saint's patience, and it was even more wearying for this child. For this child, there was neither an urge nor an ability to express his own rightness in either words or demands. In nature and in rich solitude, he found no disease of words or of conflicting desires; there was only a richly satisfying "rapport," healing in its peaceful internal harmonies and rhythms. For the child knew—although he couldn't have said it in these words—that the real correspondence is in Silence, beyond and deep within, and that the surface fluttering and ego-antics blurred this true language.

Emmanuel felt no gregarious urge, no call to join any society, organization, party, clique, creed, or "true" religion. This was not due to dislike of them so much as to the vague feeling that joining or "belonging" to one of them would seem to shut him out from the others, and perhaps he really belonged to all. He also saw that it was most often fear which made people organize and try to shut one another either in or out. He also noted that when people explained, organized, and formulated, they often dulled and deadened—ending up clinging to a stereotyped, sterile form—while the Life escaped, winged and carefree. For Emmanuel, Life had myriad forms to play in and had Eternity in its rhythm; he smiled at the ego's attempts to fix and hold it.

Ties of blood, class, race, and caste were not strong and they did not become bondage. The sharing of consciousness and living awareness seemed the most real of belongings. Emmanuel accepted the *karmic* and *dharmic* relationships that evolved among his blood people. At times, there was the nat-

11

Silence is the language of the Real.
Stillness is the requisite for the realization,
or rather,
the re-cognition of the Self as God and grace.
Grace is not a thing or quality that
we can earn, get, or possess—
it is what we ever Are.

Silence is the perfectest herald of joy:
I were but little happy if I could say how much.

—Shakespeare
Much Ado About Nothing
II, i, 319-20

ural but abortive efforts to be understood by his family-members, chiefly for the sake of their peace and quiet, to assuage their fret, their occasional craving to understand and have things "explained." What tiresome fuss! What futile trying! Trees and animals understood and did not crave, assert, or try to explain—with them, he felt the word-less exchange, the salutary rich content. Since they knew wordlessly and livingly, he would never feel lonely or lost in being alone with them. When he was drained by humans both physically and psychically, he would often seek the nearness and the touch of his tree-friends on the Viking mound, and they seemed to respond in the easy strength of Wholeness. Or did they have to give as he had to listen? Did they feel a power or a virtue leave them, as did Christ when the faithful woman secretly touched him in her quest for Wholeness.

As we in our immediate, pre-natal states have to recapitulate our previous, various physiological forms—the shapes of amoeba, fish, and animals—so the psyche has to recapitulate, in some mode or other, all its previous essential experiences and realizations. It is the quickness and relative ease in which the individual psyche re-experiences and re-realizes its past that constitutes its degree of maturity, its ripeness towards simple awareness. When games and gratifications quickly cease to satisfy, the pilgrim can make rapid progress in consciousness. We may mystically choose or at least attract our birth, our circumstances, our sufferings, and what happens to us, but that which matters most in real significance is our attitude. How do we approach what happens, perceive its message, its meaning, and its significance to us? Do we receive with simple, living acceptance or with ego-pitiful

Your everyday and ordinary consciousness—is *Tao*.
Brahman is not a particular experience,
level of consciousness,
or state of soul;
rather it is whatever level you happen
to be experiencing now.
When you realize this, it will confer upon you
a profound center of affectionate detachment
and joyous ease
that will forever persist—
even in moments of anxiety or fear,
or throughout the worst depression.

In the pursuit of learning,
every day something is added.
In the practice of the *Tao*,
every day something is dropped.
Less and less do you need to force things,
until finally you arrive at non-action.
When nothing is done,
nothing is left undone

—Lao-tzu
Tao Te Ching,
Chapter 48

Step by step as thou goeth,
the Way shall open up to thee.
Thou art the *Tao*.

resentment? Do we intuitively learn our lessons and sense our real direction?

The maturity and health of the Psyche have little to do with body age, but are closely related to *memory*. Do we recollect our Self in sincere and mystic clear vision? Do we dimly or clearly consider the whole as well as the parts? Are we aware of Eternity and of our Self in moments of degradation and darkness—or when we are feeling the pain arising from the deaths of forms and people who are loved by us? From which Center do we live? In storms and tribulations, do we retain a central balance, a sure poise, and a calm acceptance? Can we lose the "curse of property," the ease and health of our body, and the blessings and love of friends—and yet be the gainer and the lover in the Life that gives and takes?

Emmanuel's childhood conception of "God" was not very personal—it certainly was not the orthodox image of a Being outside himself with a long beard and halo. Emmanuel was not aware of any very clear distinction between Heaven, Hell, and Home. All seemed to be here—and when I was in Hell, God was there too:

> If I make my bed in Hell behold, thou art there.
> If I take the wings of the morning,
> And dwell in the uttermost parts of the sea;
> Even there shall thy hand lead me . . .[6]

When Emmanuel quickened in response to these verses,

If God didn't exist as our playmate,
He would have to be invented.
If God didn't have the Devil as play-mate,
there would be no play, no *Swa-lila*.
It is by contrasts and differences that we appreciate
God, grace, and Self,
and are made more consciously aware of Reality.

Sell your cleverness and buy bewilderment—
cleverness is mere opinion,
bewilderment is intuition.

the quickening came less from thought than from sentiments and feelings.

Emmanuel seemed more aware of the aspect of immanence than of transcendence, of Being rather than of becoming, and he did not so much walk with God, as in God, especially in his rich and ample solitude. What was most tiresome, blurring, dulling, and draining during his childhood were the noisy, assertive, and aggressive folks trying to share their ideals and their prejudices.

Although Emmanuel did not take eagerly to what was called "education" and "civilization," his consciousness had become colored by ego, and when he was 8 years old, he gradually succumbed to a sin-complex. Secretly and unbeknownst to any human but himself, Emmanuel heaved a large stone (which had been lying quietly by the roadside) on its end, so that it stood erect like a *lingam*. To him, it became quite a landmark. There it stood silently for Remembrance, a notion probably remembered from reading "Israel's dream" of an open heaven, angels ascending and descending on ladders, and of a battle with God, and a stone of Remembrance erected on the spot. The sight of the stone was to remind him of the more real mode of awareness—the essential world of living values and harmonious relationships—which was at that time in grave danger of being lost sight of in the frothy and choppy waves of usurping ego-consciousness. Ego-memories threatened to blot out *memory*, and the uplifted countenance of the good stone was to remind me: "You stupid and giddy boy! How can you forget your Self like that? Remember! Remember! and you will not laugh at such silly tricks and

Good and evil, dead and alive, everything blooms
from one natural stem.
You know this already, I'll stop.
Any direction you turn it's one vision.

—Jalāl al-Dīn Rūmī
from the poem "The Elusive Ones,"
translated by Coleman Barks

While Sri Krishna,
Himself God Incarnate,
played with the gopis at Vrindavan,
trouble-makers appeared on the scene.
You may ask why.
The answer is that they thicken the plot.
The play is enlivened by the presence of trouble-makers.
They are necessary to lend zest to the play—
there is no fun without them.

—Sri Ramakrishna

these merely clever antics. You'll not wallow in desires, nor fall for mean temptations. Remember! Recollect your Self!"

It was not so much a big "Don't" from mySelf to me as a call to Remembrance of *memory*—where beyond thoughts, there are no oughts, no conflicting desires, no divided consciousness, and no dis-ease of trying. In this unitive mode of experiencing, the idea of sin is seen to be rooted in the ignorance of our true nature. In its unitive Light, we are livingly aware that "one will is ever done on earth as in heaven." We lose the conceit of agency and know livingly that unbroken *perfectum est*. So why pray in words? Why fuss in ego-willful doings?

The Stone of Remembrance did not shout loudly enough. *Memory* became more intermittent in consciousness, and the Viking boy duly fell into the grip of desires. The clear vision and the calm grace were blurred in the play of ego-consciousness. But not entirely. Even then, there were still those very rare moments where the combination of Solitude and Silence would reawaken the Song of mySelf.

In the lucid moments of ego-forgetfulness, even grown-up children may well make the winged journey from a divided to an integral consciousness, from the outer "multi-universe" to the inward "universe." It is an effortless journey in the second as in the first innocence, in the pre-mental as in the mature, child-like state of awareness beyond both emotional waves and mental usurpation. The journey's speed is not a matter of merit, of ideals, of trying, nor of willing. Fatal both to arrival and to entrance are power-complexes, *shakti-antics*, and all the ways of ego-consciousness. But children may consciously or unconsciously harmonize their environment by

Instead of circumstances, there is *innerstances*.
Instead of understand, *innerstand*.
This I AM *innerstands*, everywhere.
Why criticize—and judge God's handiwork?
I never made any plans—
the Plan is there
and we can fit in
with joyous ease
and delightful uncertainty.

The empty vessel makes the greatest sound.

—Shakespeare
Henry V, IV, iv, 72

The Real Silence is not the absence of sound or talk,
but comes from being "desire-free."
To be "desire-free" does not mean
that desires will not arise in you,
but rather that you will not be driven by these desires.
Although you will not necessarily be free *of* desire,
you can be free *in* desire.

making circumstances and especially *innerstances* right and conducive for the necessary change to happen beautifully. Our blinkers dissolve and we are livingly free amidst the clarity of Being. Yet Emmanuel did not experience anything happening suddenly; grace arrived in the fullness of time.

The first and the second Innocence appeared to be similar, yet their immediate background was different. When we are able to accept and livingly adopt our sufferings, there is something added; so something was added in the second Innocence. It was as if the memories of a recently performed shadow-play, though faded in details, made us more aware of the Light on the screen of Silence. Because of contrasts, there was a richer acceptance, a more conscious awareness. The first Innocence was simply simple—it was pure because of the long preceding purgation and forgetting of impurities. In the second Innocence, the consciousness was pure in contrast to recent shadows and impurities whose essence still lingered nearby.

As there is always compensation in every trial and ill, so also everything has its shadows, rightly, duly, and perfectly so. We also learn to love the shadows and to accept them livingly as a due part of unbroken perfection. No person who has ever died the mystic death into Life is afraid to die out of his body. Such a fearless soul can joyfully play in both words and shadows and yet remain aware of the living Silence.

When children take up a conch or a large sea-shell, and listen to the sound within, they often have a queer, fascinating, and half-frightening sense of *memory*. A Himalayan Silence is ever singing in the mystic Sunyata Cave within each psyche. Its song is *memory*—we hear it not in the mere absence of

21

A man who seeks truth will never find it.
Truth is in what IS and that is the beauty of it.
The moment you conceptualize it,
the moment you seek it,
you become agitated,
and the man who struggles
cannot innerstand that we have to be still
to aware THAT.
I AM is always aware.

sound, but in the stilling of both desires and efforting, in the cessation of ego-consciousness.

With the advent of ego-consciousness and in the flux of surface-values, children forget. Ego-memories, desires, and willfulness blur and hide our conscious *memory* of our unitive Self and of our psychic Wholeness. But some grown-up children vaguely remember. Intuition emerges, develops, and (if practiced and trained) gradually grows too clear to ever again be blurred by the deceptions and disguises of false values. These are seen through, and the soul is no longer confused by them. Once intuition is no longer permitted to atrophy unused, ignored, and discredited, it becomes a serviceable, trust-worthy tool.

In our maturity, this realization grew clearer and the *memory* of Self appeared as the only Real one. We no longer appeared to be entombed in the tools of body, mind, and thought—which Socrates pointed out could "imprison us like an oyster in its shell." It was easy to get away from the memories of past glories and sins, to merge the sub- and super-consciousness, and to have no thought of the future. Even as the days passed, we would be livingly aware of Eternity. The light of the Whole would reveal its beautiful differences, and awarely we would play in the changing *lila*. Without our even trying, conflicts and problems would both resolve and dissolve, and the Universe would again become what it ever Is—we are simply aware.

In Silence, we close our outward eyes and our clever minds to perceptions. Then within ourSelves awakens *memory*—the power of steady vision and clear Remembrance

23

Sri *Wuji* says:
"Thou shalt not kill."
If body, mind, and ego
are viewed as the useful and necessary tools
through which we function,
then we need no longer try to kill them.
When we do not identify our Self
with these bodies and tools,
we are body-free, mind-free, and ego-free.

of what we Are, the birthright of all. Then we no longer need a guide—for we live at ease, at Home as artists in Life. The dis-ease of assertion and trying is healed and eased by Silence.

One thousand years B.C., the Sages of Egypt proclaimed: "O, Thou sweet well for him that thirsteth in the desert! It is closed to him who speaketh, but open to him who is Silent. When who is Silent cometh, lo! he findeth the well."

And the ancients of Tibet knew: "The mind is the slayer of the Real, let the disciple slay the slayer. Kill in thyself all memories of past experiences. Look not behind, or thou art lost."

Yet why slay or kill? The real cannot be slain, only obscured, and we need not kill the poor memories. Let them die simply and naturally. They do fade and cease to be bondage when they are seen as they are, as illusions and toys. Look not behind with longing, glee, or attachment, or we are lost like Mrs. Lot,[7] lost in thought and stuck in the bondage of memories. Consciousness is held in bonds by love of things, and so it cannot proceed and clarify into awareness, in which there is an end to longings, yearnings, and efforting. No more do "we look before and after and grieve for what is not." Past and future merge into the At-Homeness of the Eternal Now. All our striving, all *yoga* practices, and all becoming and "begoing" seem to be conscious or unconscious attempts to clarify the mirror of the soul, to be sine-cere[8]; once we learn to reflect purely and thus to transcend the dis-ease of ego-consciousness, we have our being in the harmonious ease of simple living Awareness. Within *memory* is the essence of all memories. And is not the only real progress, the only true becoming

Do not complain
or cry
or pray,
but open
your intuitive
Shiva-eye
and
apperceive.

Things have to happen.
The only thing we can do
is to change our attitude toward them.
It makes a lot of difference whether
you accept things or you don't.

in our Being—being more and more aware of our *memory*, of our Self?

The earliest seven years of rich loneliness were broken by the impact of assertive, desireful fellow-pilgrims, or rather Emmanuel's attempt to vibrate harmoniously with them. Ego dis-ease was rampant. There was really very little bullying, benevolent or otherwise; no regimentation, no forcing into conformity, except that of an "enlightened democracy." But the mere presence of mental, emotional and matter-blinkered fellow-pilgrims impinged on him. He could no longer shut them out of his consciousness, but had to attune to their vibration and thereby—at least for the moment—become them. The Silence and the Wholeness was thus limited by the noisy rhythms and the assertive concerns of individuals. Emmanuel did not consciously resent or object, yet he did not seek company, and instinctively he avoided the dis-harmonious and the forceful. Emmanuel did not go out gladly, not even to learn to be taught or to be improved. Not one of the grown-ups seemed to see or to talk to him. Do we ever "see" children? How can we with our mental blinkers and ego-values? We teach and talk at them or love them in our own image. Inevitably so, but to Emmanuel the limitation was often trying and tiresome. Only in safe Solitude did he feel free to unfold, to heal, and to Be.

After the Jewish Yahweh had created the world (earth,

It is all a mattter of maturity.
We can't make ourselves more mature,
but we can accept
our immaturity.

Be sincere and patient—and remember the Self.
Forgetfulness of the Self is the source of all misery.

Whatsoever happens, happens—
and I have no judgment,
no desire that it should be different.
All is right that seems most wrong (to clever egojies).
Awaken to aware the Divine All-Rightness,
the unbroken perfection that is in and over all.

heaven, and hell), "He saw that it was good." But that was before He created man after his own likeness and, as an afterthought, from one of the poor man's ribs, created the division we call woman. This does not imply that we are born in "sin" or by mistake, but rather that humans, as individuals, all have the fatal tendency to fall into ego-consciousness in their early childhood. Only some idiots and a few pure fools escape lightly from that infantile disease, and unlike measles, most of us suffer from it in acute or chronic form until the release of death. Ego-consciousness—by keeping us in a feverish delirium—prevents us from experiencing those lucid moments of Silence that would enable us to unfold our wings and fly away from worldly worries. Ego-life itself is a form of death shutting us off from both the awareness of Life and the true Self-identification. So very few seem to outgrow it and to fall out of the illusion of the fatal division of Me and Thee, or to forget the illusory strutting I! I! I! business.

In due time came the impact of school and play-mates. Grown-up children tried to inform and reform, to improve and to "progress" Emmanuel's consciousness of values and of truth. Duly they tried to impose their duty-complexes, sin-complexes, and mental blinkers; but in this attempt to mould him into their ideal image, they met with less than average success. The sensitive, passive, and receptive boy—after all—did not prove to be a good medium, but neither was he felt to be a bad nor an impossible one. He complied passively and conscientiously, but not eagerly. These things apparently had to be done, and a promise, also an exacted one, had to be kept and paid like a debt, but there was no enthusing, no

29

Intellect is not intelligence,
knowledge is not Wisdom,
ananda is not mere happiness.

The endless cycle of idea and action,
Endless invention, endless experiment,
Brings knowledge of motion, but not of stillness;
Knowledge of speech, but not of silence;
Knowledge of words, and ignorance of the Word.

Where is the life we have lost in living?
Where is the wisdom we have lost in knowledge?
Where is the knowledge we have lost in information?

—T.S. Eliot
Choruses from 'The Rock', (1934)

gushing, and few assertive demands. So he was little noticed and probably considered to be very average. His silence was the cloak of invisibility, and if he was noticed, it would be as a quiet, kindly, passive, unassertive, dull, but rather harmless boy; a true child of both my earthly and heavenly fathers.

What a blessing it was in my case to be unnoticed and to be let be. It may be true charity, courtesy, dignity, and love to let children Be; we let them discover their own truth by not trying to inspire them, "do them good," or by imposing our own truth over them, at them, and for them. Their truth may be different—beautifully different—and our business is to live our own truth. All that glitters is not gold, and the Golden Rule—"Do unto others as you would be done by"—might on certain levels be amended. Their needs may be different.

Egoism has many strange disguises. Through subtle ego-deceptions, we may well crucify the virtue and drain the Life-flow out of our beloved ones by our so seemingly unegoistical eagerness to share, to help, to inspire, to guide, and to love them. "They do not know what they do." Egos cannot aware their own Self—nor the Self in others—and their eager trying must be forgiven.

My native passive positivity and the calm sense of imma-nence do not seem to be characteristic of the average, Western-born psyche, but it is still not so uncommon in *Jutland*. Even if the *Jutes* are Vikings, they have out-grown the infantile and adolescent lust for external power through conquest. There, the white man's (or pure Aryan) burden is a thing of the past. Now their victories are within, and one of their proverbs is: "What outwardly we lost, we can inwardly win." There are

Thus shall ye think of all this fleeting world:
a star at dawn,
a bubble in a stream,
a flash of lightning on a summer cloud,
a flickering lamp,
a phantom,
and
a dream.

—Vajracchedikă Prajñāpāramita Sūtra

conquests more valid, vital, and real than the juvenile ones of war; as we've seen so many times this century, wars require the brutalization and vulgarization of fellow-pilgrims, the propaganda of hero-worship and the gory-glory of radio, movies, and daily press-power. A real victor may be crowned with an inner glory, unseen and unknown to the noisy and clever ones. Since his freedom is not seen by egos, they can neither give to it nor take away from it. He may pass through the country and through "what ye call life" unnoticed and unenvied, without disturbing anybody or anything, leaving no trace, as a fish through the water or as a bird through the air. Both he and his artistic expression may blend into the landscape and not stand out against it. His wordless acceptance is his art, his freedom, and his power—this is the power which needs neither recognition nor advertisement, and the language of this power is Silence.

Deeper and deeper the Viking-boy descended into ego-consciousness. Desires and power-politics over-shadowed the Light of the Real, and the play was on the surface. "We are such stuff as dreams are made of."[9] Dreams within dreams. Illusions within plays of illusions. The center seemed to have shifted and, more and more, the actual and the factual were called reality. Eternity receded in the play of time.

Father never asserted nor preached in words. He was a wordless mystic, who simply was. In regard to the rightness

Our revels now are ended. These our actors,
As I foretold you, were all spirits and
Are melted into air, into thin air;
And, like the baseless fabric of this vision,
The cloud-capp'd towers, the gorgeous palaces,
The solemn temples, the great globe itself,
Yea, all which it inherit, shall dissolve;
And, like this insubstantial pageant faded,
Leave not a rack behind. We are such stuff
As dreams are made of, and our little life
Is rounded with a sleep.

—With respects to Shakespeare
The Tempest, IV, i, 148-158

Dreams are true while they last,
and do we not live in dreams?

—Alfred, Lord Tennyson
in the poem
"The Higher Pantheism" (1869)

of fellow-pilgrims who vibrated in a different and even contrary rhythm, he lived his truth with the least possible fuss and interference. Mother both talked and asserted her feminine truth, and the usual subtly willful *shakti-business* in her rhythm, but it was neither vicious nor persistent. She could also be clear and silent and still.

The feminine elements happened to be the most vocal and most playful on the surface of things in my childhood setting. The women vibrated noisily and I came to accept them and learned their language, which is spoken and lived by half of our humanity. Two grown up sisters, 12 and 14 years older in body than I, were not "remembered" until I was about 7, though they must have been an unconscious influence. There was the managing mother and a succession of servant-girls (farmers' daughters and considered by my mother our "equals"). As I was not very conscious of sexual differences, for me there was no war of the sexes.

In Viking land, there was co-education and sex equality in sharing, play, and work. Although the males were rarely found to be rearing children, preparing meals, or serving food, and the women joined the miniature army only as healers and nurses, there was widespread sex equality. So from childhood, the feminine rhythm was no more strange to me than was the masculine one, different in quality but not in kind, and each individual rhythm varied. I saw each person as a beautifully different variation of the same Life. At school we all shared in games and in lessons, and at home we shared in work and in leisure. At one time a neighboring girl (also a late and lonely child) was often my play-fellow, and for years a city-boy was

Never the Spirit was born.
The Spirit shall cease to be—never.
Never was the time it was not.
Ends and beginnings are dreams.
Birthless and deathless and changeless
remaineth the Spirit—
forever.
Death hath not touched It at all,
dead though the form,
the house of IT—seems.

—With respects to Sir Edwin Arnold,
from Chapter II of *The Song Celestial*,
his translation of the *Bhagavad Gita*

my intimate companion on the farm.

And so it happened that I was not conscious of any great difference between the male and the female rhythms, which in other lands seems not only to be different in degree, but also of kind and species. There were no clashes in the household because Father did not react impatiently or violently, and was not easily provoked; he was easy in humoring whims, yet firm and steadfast in his own Self when essential and important decisions had to be made. He had the generosity of strength, and rarely fought and argued; are not most of our squabbles due to weakness and to ignorance of the Self?

It did not then occur to me that there is a feminine truth, complementary, but often contrasting and seemingly at war with the masculine truth. The division was not clear in my consciousness. Truly, I felt that the girls and women around me were often more noisy with their tongues and desires than were the boys and men, more emotional, more volatile, more silly, but also more gentle, sensitive, and feeling. Vicariously I lived in their feminine rhythms, vibrating with them in unitive, direct, and un-mental harmonies. I was no stranger to their subtly willful passive waiting—similar to a cat lying in wait for a mouse—nor to their seemingly insincere play and poses, the flutter and the wordiness, which often hides their true purpose and meaning. Intuitively and vibrationally, I came to "know" the feminine language of being, though I myself had no desire to speak it. Often I "knew" women better than they knew themselves (so they said), yet I could not myself take a pose or play a part which was not my own. I was uncritical, unanalytical, receptive, and accepting—and

Take no thought for the morrow.
Sufficient unto the day is that day's own content.
Live spontaneously in the present—the Eternal Now.
The intuitive Light will reveal Reality.

—With respects to Jesus
Matthew 6:34

Desire no-thing,
possess no-thing,
will no-thing.

All craving is due to a sense of insufficiency.
When you aware that YOU lack nothing—
that is,
YOU are being—awareness—grace—
then your desires, cravings, and yearnings cease
and there is nothing to practice;
to BE your Self,
stop imagining yourself to be this or that,
just BE.

yet (somehow), when in danger, aware. With women, I did have an intuitive flair which saved me from the scratches of the claws hidden behind their velvety pussy feet. I was perhaps not always conscious of the danger at the moment it was happening, but then would be afterwards when I developed the negatives in the inner darkroom of my consciousness. Intuition preceded and predominated and could (nearly always) be trusted.

Is not the highest type of manhood really that which includes womanhood? Are not the feminine and the masculine rhythms complementary? When the complementary opposite rhythms are harmonized and functioning at ease within, the individual can be calmly aware of his Individuum. As the Bible says: ". . . and they shall again become one flesh."

He seemed to be only half a man—a prey to fluctuations and golden chains—who had to search and to lean on a "better half" for his fulfillment or Wholeness. And she but half a woman who—finding her support and fulfillment outside herself—attracts or is attracted to a worse half to bully or to obey. In the ancient garden of pure consciousness, two falls occurred: the first was when man was divided and woman formed from his lost rib; and this caused and conditioned the second—when both became self-critical and "saw that they were naked" and divided, and so descended into the play of opposites. Good and evil for what?

Aesthetically, the hermaphrodite is a type of perfection, an idea or truth, which has haunted the imagination of men like Michelangelo, Shelley, and Whitman. Physiologically, we all still have the rudiments of the other sex; we have developed from some hermaphroditic organism in the dim past,

I am not whole unless I am alone—
then there is no "other".

There are no others—
there is only wrong identification of the Self
with the senses, the body, and the mind.

The strongest man (woman) is he (she)
who stands Alone.

Aloneness
can be
all-one-ness.

Sri Wuji in the invisible Real says:
"YourSelf and mySelf are identical—*samata*.
I know this, but *egojies* do not.
This is all the difference and it cannot last."

40

and it may be that we are being carried along to some hermaphroditic fulfillment in the not too far-off future. Meanwhile, those among us to whom the time-scale is not of supreme importance, can have glimpses and sensations of these past and future states in the present, the Eternal Now. Perhaps we cannot stay calm and balanced in unitive modes of experiencing unless that harmonious, hermaphroditic Wholeness is achieved within. We meet physically hermaphroditic types among fellow pilgrims. Are they reversions, freaks, or hints of future perfection? Even though now they are often pitied, soon they may be envied.

Physique, however, is not so important as that which is much vaster—the psyche. The hermaphroditic psyche seems to be the one thing most necessary for inner peace. How easy it would be to avoid the war of the sexes and the agonies of readjustment if our psyches were whole and did not need to flutter in search of their other halves, their lost integral Wholeness! How easy to eliminate fears and jealousies, the efforts to bind and to possess—if only the individual could find within himSelf or herSelf that pearl of great prize: the *memory* of what and of who we really Are!

Within is the "kingdom"—and only there can we again find our lost Harmony, our psychic Wholeness. It can never be found outside of ourselves; and any search outside ourselves will only lead to compulsive *shakti* busy-ness. Love of humanity, nation, society, race, family, mate, or even the beloved can only lead to an extension of a divided and dual ego-consciousness. To lose one's ego in anything other than the Self can only produce an ego that is both enlarged and inflated. Only within his or her own psyche, beyond ego-con-

41

What is a religious man?
I will tell you what a religious man is.
First of all, a religious man is a man who is Alone—
not lonely, you understand,
but Alone—
with no theories or dogmas, no opinion, no background;
he is alone and enjoying it.
Secondly, a religious man must be both man and woman—
I don't mean sexually—
but he must be aware of the dual nature of everything;
a religious man must feel and be
both masculine and feminine.

—With respects to J. Krishnamurti
(The question in the first line
was put to Krishnamurti by
Laura Huxley, as recorded in
her book *This Timeless Moment*.)

sciousness, can a person know him or herself to be as simple and as Whole as Adam and Eve before the fall—but now with the added remembrance of a shadow which makes the Light at the Center of consciousness richer than it ever was before.

The growing pains in overcoming the disease of divided consciousness are richly rewarded. The causes for all that happens to us are within ourselves, and we need never blame anybody or anything outside for our miseries. Probably we cannot experience the Natural State unless we are momentarily psychically whole—nor can we retain it livingly unless we remain so. This rhythm of inner psychic wholeness is what egos would term "androgynous." When the male and the female truths function in a complementary harmony within one psyche, the body (as a tool) will remain male or female, but the psyche will aware the harmonious wholeness of itSelf, freely functioning in the unitive mode of experiencing.

Only in the Light of the Whole can *memory* emerge freely, simply, and purely; and is not the (conscious or unconscious) aim and purpose, meaning and goal of all of our strivings, all our *shakti-antics*, and all our yoga practices to be aware and to remain aware of our integral Wholeness, the hermaphrodite androgyne, the mystically united twin within our Self? The magic force in the golden unitive thread of intuitive *memory* reveals to us our Self, and leads and draws us onward with *dharmic* speed to the Beyond (which is within) of Eternity's ever-present Sunrise.

I have never said there is no God.
I have said there is only God as manifested in you.
I prefer to call it Life.
I am not concerned with society,
with religion,
with dogma,
but I am concerned with Life—
because I AM Life.

—J. Krishnamurti

Many new dialects and languages came into the ken of this Viking boy, and he listened and learned. In the instinctual mode of early childhood, he attuned himself to the living rhythms of the trees, the birds, and the animals. He felt depleted when noisy people encroached with their assertive explanations and with ideas, ideals, and prejudices—all in various desire-vibrations. He would become wearied with all these humans so filled with bubbling desires, effervescent ego-willfulness, and vital ego-antics! Even if each individual had a language of her or his own, a vibrational and unconscious one, in comparison with nature, they all seemed noisy, assertive, and tiresome.

It was not that I was critical and analytical in attitude, nor too consciously wearied to know the cause of my frequent depletion. Humans were accepted as a form of Life, but while the organic language of nature did not disturb or drain my Silence, the noisy, willful language of the "unnatural" humans caught and held my attention and put silence and unitive awareness in abeyance. I "saw" vibrationally and instinctually rather than in conscious sympathy. If I was violated by others, its source was almost unconscious to me, and utterly so to the emotional and mental "intruders." Their rhythms were accepted as part of Life, and if they were not enthusiastically embraced, they were at least tolerated and endured.

So I listened vibrationally, and vicariously lived thousands of lives. I learnt the diverse languages of fellow beings, and the various rhythms in which Life expressed itSelf through them. There was no wish to speak the language of other fellow-pilgrims, as this would have felt false to me, nor was there any urge to find a way to express myself through words.

45

Unto the pure, all things are pure.

—St. Paul
The Epistle of Paul to Titus 1:15

I have learned in whatsoever state I AM,
therewith to be content.

—St. Paul
The Epistle of Paul to the Philippians 1:21

Some languages were interesting, others seemed dull, but listening and learning were useful kinds of disciplines, conducive to flexibility, tolerance, and patience. Was it not St. Paul who suffered fools gladly? One may suffer even intellectuals gladly. All Life is loveable if it can be viewed as an ever changing form. The wearisomeness to a passive listener is in the repetition and sameness of the surface-play, of oft-told reminiscences—which is like a record on a gramophone going on and on and on. One has no choice but to attend to it. It is no use trying to ignore it or withdraw attention. The whole psychic body of the passive soul is open and exposed, and cannot concentrate or shut out the noise.

Interest deepened when I realized that only my mind need listen to the surface play of word-language—while I could attune to sensing the vibrations below and beyond—in the language of Being. I quickly saw that most often wordy explanations were the conscious or unconscious disguises for the feelings hidden underneath.

Vibrationally, vicariously, and intuitively, I could momentarily live the lives of thousands of fellow-pilgrims, and could know, not only their fleeting moods and antics, but their depths. Through Silence, empathy, compassion, and by becoming them vibrationally (if only for a moment), I could know them livingly. It felt like this "knowing" by identity was the true knowledge of egos and of psyches, and it also revealed the unity between fellow-pilgrims and all other forms of Life.

I saw that trying was of no use. It was fatal for Self-knowledge, for with my efforts and attempts, there crept in the desires and attachments that blurred my inner vision. But in

The Light that never was on land or sea
and which enlightens and guides every ego
that enters this world-play
is awared intuitively in your Self,
if you mature and purify your tools to reflect purity.

If thine intuitive eye be single, clear, and whole,
thy whole body
—(aye, all bodies)—
will be awared, intuited, and experienced
as brimful of Self-Radiant Light
(the Light that never was on sea or land—but ever Is).

—With respects to Jesus
Matthew 6:22;
(the line about "the Light that
never was on sea or land"
is taken from Wordsworth's
Elegiac Stanzas, stanza 4)

48

pure passivity and in Silence, the consummation just was. Only when the muddy water of the mind was let be and the choppy waves of the emotions were stilled could the mirror of the lake effortlessly reflect that which I vainly tried to see and to know. I could know livingly and vibrationally through Self-identification.

It is well to be able to go in and to go out of consciousness calmly, balancedly, stilly. In the deepest sense, the Real—which is also the All, the Everything, and the No-thing—is within. That which conceives, recollects and recognizes the Self outside is already within or else there could be no re-cognition, no conceiving. But many individuals seemed to only be able to play through the extroverted modes of ego-antics and power politics—and then their only rest from this frenzied assertion would be through the surface-waves of words.

When in childhood I retreated from playing, it was often to a liberating sense of ease and of right relatedness, and to a glad inward feeling of being warmly welcomed to healing, living harmonies. Photographic plates changed after contemplation; in the dark cave Within, the pictures became clear or even vanished. Were the memories, the contacts, and the correspondences valid and vital enough when exposed to a calm and still light? Were they worthwhile repeating? Should they be treasured through re-experiencing—or could the pictures be put into the waste-basket of oblivion? Had they real content and meaning or were they idle and trivial shadow-plays? From the vantage point of *memory*, the feverish assertions and eager ego-antics (both my own and others) would seem futile, evanescent, and tiresome—a queer dis-ease that had to be silently accepted and lived through. As long as we are addict-

Truth cannot be achieved or possessed by the ego.
We cannot realize (i.e. make Real) that which is ever Real.
When you recognize that you are **not** a person,
but a pure and calm witnessing,
that your very being is pure awareness—
then you will be at the source.

Even if in common parlance,
it is usually said that the opposite of death is life,
this is a false notion that derives
from the all-pervasive fear of death.
If death had an opposite, it would be birth;
just as every death results in a birth,
and every birth in a death,
so who we **are**
is eternal life.
Life has no opposite and its secret is death.

Awake to aware that you are enlightened
and have ever been so.

ed to the joys of playing on the surface-*lila*, the only "time-out" from the wear and tear of our learned ignorance is the rest we call sleep and the sleep we call death.

The dream of life lasts a little longer than does the dream of sleep, but both are unreal. The less we are aware of Eternity, Memory, Silence, and the Life that comprises birth and death, the more deaths do we need. The mystery of how a unified consciousness can become double is as subtle as the mysteries of creation and growth. In my case, "the fall" was a gradual affair and ego-consciousness only clipped the wings of *memory* after a prolonged period of time.

In my rhythm, there was but little urge to mentalize, analyze, understand, or assert what I "knew." Because there were so few conflicts, the growing ego was not truculent nor pugnacious, and had few ambitions or even goals. In solitude, there was little opposition and so little chance of growing a robust ego; and until the physical age of 14—in spite of school and people—I had a good deal of solitude at work and at play. There was no loneliness in solitude and work was a kind of play.

The play within was only slightly imaginative, fanciful, or dreamy—it was a living, unitive whole, a contemplative non-duality where all of life was playfully experienced. In my usual mode of being, I was not broody, nor stilled in meditation, nor fixed in concentration, nor busy in puzzling things out. There was a freedom which was neither introverted nor extroverted; there were thought-feelings rather than thoughtfulness, and, at times, the unitive awareness beyond thought and beyond desires. All other modes were there intermittently, but solitude was the one in which I felt most at home, suffused

The very desire for awareness prevents it.
There can be no preparation for that which always IS.
To aware Truth, Reality, God, Self, needs no preparation.
Preparation implies time,
and time is **not** the means of comprehending truth.
Truth is time-free.

Suffering is due to non-acceptance.
When pain is accepted for what it is—
a lesson and a warning—
and deeply looked into and heeded,
the separation between pain and pleasure breaks down;
both become experience,
painful when resisted, joyful when accepted.

—Sri Nisargadatta Maharaj
I Am That,
dialogue 59

by healing Wholeness and harmonious Silence.

If the noisy ones could have seen my solitude, they might have termed me "dreamy"; but as they could not aware this side of me, I appeared to them—though not ambitious nor brilliant—sufficiently attentive, responsive, and practical. I was a fairly good listener, even to tedious tales, patient of ego-antics, tolerant of frailty and foibles, uncondemning of blunders and of "sins." I had a certain calm balance both in success and in calamities, no fuss or flutter, but a practical simplicity in making the best of all situations. I was simple, economical, and anti-waste.

When—at the bodily age of 11 or 12—I was at a party with other children, there occurred an instance of concurrent dual consciousness. We were romping around like any other young animal, and suddenly in the midst of the game, I experienced myself as being also outside it. I continued to play, but was apart from it. What happened was a double consciousness. I saw—subjectively—my body and the other players and the game progressing, but concurrently I also saw the actors—objectively—as if they were being driven by a force of which they thought themselves masters. I saw them as the egos known by name and form as they thought they were, and also—vibrationally—as they really were . And the thoughts came to me: "What are we all doing? We are being used—by what? What is the meaning of it all?"

Although my "Soul" was no longer in the game, part of me

We obscure the Self
with thoughts and symbols that divide and clash.
We cannot handle pain or fear by avoiding it,
but only through realizing that we ARE it.

Rejoice in gratitude—
and endure patiently what you cannot enjoy.

continued to play and to talk quite ordinarily, though in a queer wistful mood—as if I was on automatic. Soon, one of the boys seemed to notice me psychically. He was a year my junior and I am sure we shared in this see-change. A wordless look and a later question from him made me certain—we were both momentarily "open" and doubly aware.

In my 14th year, the world around and within crashed. The farm—my outside world—was sold to and desecrated by strangers, and from that time on I felt uprooted, or perhaps more deeply at home within. I discovered both my wings and my roots. Later on, although I loved my various homes, I was able to make myself at home everywhere: it was easy for me to be a traveler as I was unattached to a special place or to a particular home. Life was a pilgrimage; I felt that I—like a snail—brought along with me my real home, my shell or shield of Silence. Also at 14, adolescence began to play havoc with *memory*, and the exoteric structure of religious forms and dogmas—that were taught to me and imposed upon me—unravelled, and all was a tangle, a chaos. Even in this chaos of consciousness, there were vivid gleams and calm recollections of *memory*, and the awareness of this Light lessened the confusion.

From the age of 7 till 14, ego-consciousness was developed as a kind of self-defense or as a reflection of the mentality and the ego-desires of the humans around me. Though it had strong and subtle roots within, ego was also provoked, fostered, and developed by much tuning in and listening to the rhythms and vibrations of fellow-pilgrims. The ego was invoked as a reflex in self-defense, but in the same process, it was also humbled, crucified, and crushed. Many a time it crumbled, and these were

Where can I go to, I AM always here.
If there is pain, let it be;
it is also the Self
and
the Self is *purnam*—
complete, whole, perfect.

—Ramana Maharshi

Spiritual suffering is a contradiction in term-symbols;
spirit doth not suffer;
suffering is not spiritual—
though it may lead to spiritual awakening and awareness.

A Death blow is a Life blow to Some
Who till they died, did not alive become—
Who had they lived, had died but when
They died, Vitality begun.

—Emily Dickinson
Poem 816
(composed in 1864)

valuable experiences. It was exactly what the illusory ego—strutting around in its bloated power-complexes, *shakti-antics*, and conceit of agency—needed to have happen; after being humbled, crucified, and crushed many a time, it died naturally. Death is the secret of ego-free living.

There is no wooden cross, except as a symbol. The cross of ego-life suffices until we remain on it long enough to regain our psychic Wholeness. This implies the dissolving of ego. "Spiritual suffering" is a contradiction in term symbols—just as is "assertive culture." There is nothing spiritual about suffering; and the Spirit cannot suffer. It is our identification with the illusory ego and with the mere reflection, which we call mind, which must be crushed, expunged, and outgrown. The whole does not assert.

Due to my passive receptivity and *negative capability*,[10] (both marvelous tools, but each also having a shadow side that made me seem weak), there was a steady succession of "smaller" ego crucifixions as I made contact with people during childhood. But wounds, lacerations, and repressions were often healed in the concurrent flow of solitude in which lived Dr. Harmony and Sri Silence. There, as the bruised ego ceased to will and assert, thoughts could rest and hurts could heal.

All thoughts are an extroverted activity of the mind, and the mind is extroverted until it reflects the Self purely. Once you can still your thoughts, they will no longer blur *memory*. Transcend ego-consciousness and be Self-Aware.

Later on, there were "bigger" crucifixions that were not easy, but—mercifully—they were brief. Dying also became more easy once it was a habit. After an adolescent love was

Die before you die.

—Mohammed

thwarted, the realization came—clearly and fairly lastingly—
that it is our love which makes us rich. The light that I loved
in my Beloved was like light shining forth from a lantern; I saw
that it was the light that I loved and not the lantern. The light
of the beloved might seem to no longer be shining, but having
once seen it, I realized that the light would be there forever.

I came to see that the essence of love is not reciprocity,
reward, nor requital; not touch, gratification, possessive joys,
nor ego-fulfillment, but just this steady seeing and contemplation of the ever living Beauty that is, and which is "ours" to the
degree to which we can appreciate that which is deepest in our
Self. The beauty that we see around us is really only within our
own psyche. That which re-cognizes itSelf is within.

Outside friends would console and commiserate: "It is
painful, but it will pass; we have been through it and can sym-
pathize with you; cheer up—there are still as many good fish
in the sea as ever came out of it." And so the ego-Play could
go on glibly, and the same grievances, the same complications,
and the same ego-pity recur.

What is better than gushing sympathy as we fussily attempt
to bandage the wounds of our fellow-pilgrim is assisting them
to help themselves; by our example, we can teach them to look
within for the cause of their trouble and grievances. How we
fuss and gush in our grievance-complexes! How we analyze
and retell our symptoms! Our psychic diseases are often clearly reflected in the diseases of our physical, emotional, and
mental tools, but symptoms are mistaken for the cause. Within
ourselves is the Source of the healing of nations, and also within is the healing (or acceptance) of our physical, emotional,

Do not give your love—it may get lost.
Radiate it like the sun.

Do not complain—or cry—or pray,
but open your intuitive *Shiva-eye*
and apperceive that the Light is all around you
(and within),
and It is so marvelous, so beautiful, so wonderful,
and so far beyond anything that you have ever imagined,
prayed for, or even dreamt of—
and It is—
for ever and ever.
Though our sun and all the other star-suns
were to become extinct,
still the Source of life would bubble on
as eternally as it does.

Heaven calls you and revolves around you,
showing you its everlasting beauty,
and your eye perceives only the passing earth.

—Dante Alighieri
Purgatorio,
Canto XIV, lines 148-150

and mental diseases. Rather than lean on the love and advice of other fellow-pilgrims, see if you can take your hurts and difficulties within. Let the Silence solve and heal and clarify. Who knows better than yourSelf the real cause and the real cure? Within, we may realize the meaning of our pains and our diseases, while all fellow-pilgrims usually do is to try to heal the symptoms and to console the ego. Such sympathy and kindness may prevent us from learning the lesson that could cure us.

Later on, with an expanded psyche, the different world-religions with their various hues and terms and rhythms seemed to be but different accents and changing emphases in exoteric modes of the One free and immanent Life, sometimes called God. God is one. Life—which comprises the birth and death of bodies and egos—is also one. Only expressions and dialects vary in their beautiful differences. Why should we quarrel on our way home because our prejudices are not the same?

I was wearied by exoteric dogmas, theological disputes, and mental subtleties. Wordiness and assertions soon became tiresome, and only Silence seemed completely clear and satisfying. I realized that this Silence was the esoteric heart of all religions. If religion was to be experienced—rather than argued, dissected, analyzed, or even "explained"—the test of a person's faith was not what they professed to believe, but rather how they lived. Personally, I felt no need of ritual, imagery, magic, or even of a language of symbols. The mystic Silence was the satisfying

Before Abraham was, I AM.

—*John* 8:58

The son of God, I also am, or was—
And if I was, I am: relation stands.

—John Milton
Paradise Regained (1671),
Book 4, 518-19

This man, Jesus, became so transparent by purification,
that the Univeral Christ of God
could express Itself through him
more clearly than through any man
in the Western world
of whom we have record.
Still this Son of God
—or perfect thought of infinite Spirit—
is shining in degrees
from every being in the universe.

The cross on Golgatha—thou lookest to in vain
if not within thySelf it be set up again.
If Christ a thousand times in Bethlehem was born—
and not within thySelf—it is forlorn.

—Angelus Silesius,
17th century German mystic

medium: the Silence of desire and thought. In the freedom of solitude, God was clearly immanent. God simply was, and contented me, unhidden by ideas, unblurred by words. I did not think of or to God. All was real and simple and—in this mystic clarity—there was no trying to explain or to understand the mystery of being and of becoming, the strange (but utterly harmonious) urges to live and to die. In that childhood unitive mode of experiencing God, the one Life was awared as comprising all the changing forms; in that mode of being, there were no problems, no questions, no fears—as these only pertain to egos.

No wonder that with such *memory*, I resented the narrow dogmatic and didactic preaching of the "holy" parson who tried to "bully" me into his faith. He had the language of the letter, but not that of the living Silence. This parson had the outer authority, the learning, the office, and the force of willfulness, but the local farmers around did not seem impressed by the spirit of his living. His violent tempers and intolerant criticisms might well have been relieved and released by simple understanding and living acceptance.

Against this well-meaning, flaming pillar of faith, the Viking-boy was thrust at the age of 14, and the impact had blessed results, though the encounter itself was a painful rather than pleasant one. That compulsory bullying caused this young lad to revolt. **I had to think**—and the whole fabric of dogmas and churchianity began to unravel. If I successfully loosened a knot at one place, there was sure to be a tangle elsewhere.

I seemed unable to be taught, unable to accept livingly as faith for myself, what was merely told and asserted from out-

The term-symbol **"the kingdom of heaven"**
is very vague—
so I translate that as **"the realm of grace."**
"Grace" we have a little inkling of;
we have seen certain people in "grace"—
or have been there ourselves.

Seek, find, aware and experience ye first
the inner realm of grace—
that which never can pass or change—
and all (mere) things shall be added unto you
(all that you really need).

—With respects to Jesus
Matthew 6:33

That which changes is not real enough.

side. Such mode and such language might be true and right for others, but was not felt to be mine. The effort that would be required to either understand matters of faith or to impress others with my outward show of learning never seemed important to me. What mattered most was the mystic death into Life, of the "Kingdom" here and now.

I remember responding to the "holy" parson by thinking to myself: "Know ye not that ye must be born again? The ear of corn, unless it falls unto the earth and dies, cannot live. Thou fool! That which you soweth is not quickened unless it dies. I live, yet not I, but Christ in me."

But the parson's explanations and comments bewildered me, and perhaps it showed, for he would pounce especially on me. I had to "explain," meaning he would often choose me to repeat his explanations. I muttered and fluttered and stuttered, having no word language in which I could suggest to my tormentor that our ego-consciousness hides our Self-awareness, and that we must first wake up from the deathly sleep of ignorance—of false Self-identification—before we can quicken into steady living Awareness.

Unfortunately Pastor Gudme's stern bullying and his loud facile wordiness soon shut me up, and his interpretations prevailed as the Truth. He thundered hell-fire at me when I quoted, "Seek ye the Kingdom within." "Within what?" he bellowed. Shakingly but unsubdued, I suggested, "Within all things." But he was quite sure the devil was within me prompting me to express such wicked, pantheistic notions. He preached and bullied like any dictator, but not at all subtly and suavely like a Jesuit. Although I resented it at the time, I now have come to

Whatsoever you have done to the least among you,
that have ye also done unto me.

—Emmanuel, the indwelling Christ
Matthew 25:40

To thine own Self be true
and it must follow—
as the night the day—
thou canst not then be false to any man (nor woman).
They are all the Self.

—With respects to Polonius and Shakespeare
Hamlet I, iii, 78-80

see his sternness and willfulness as a blessing—even if his hell-fire did not convince me of his doctrines and dogma, he did confirm me in my own faith.

At that time, I had no word language for this faith. But somehow I knew that "my" God was very still, positive, imma-nent—and somehow akin to feeling good, rich, and vast in the harmony of the unbroken Perfection. No words, no names, and no trying were required when I was alone, and there was rarely any need either to express or to reveal myself in words to others. But fellow-pilgrims would assert and explain noisily in con-fusing names and terms. God was certainly in my beloved trees, in the farm-animals, in the fields, and in the changing moods of nature, perhaps even more whole and dignified in these non-human friends—it was only my human "friends" who would try to fill me with their explanations, their analyzes, and their advice on how I could "progress." My God could be "Silent in seven languages" and could be still in Being, as well as busy doing things.

The term "God" more than sufficed when I was richly alone in the All. I also found that it sufficed when talking to others—it was conveniently vague and short and ambiguous, and it meant to each individual exactly what they wanted it to mean—as long as they didn't ask me to explain myself. "Each to his own Christ." On the universal path, each of us has their own *dharma*, their own true rhythm, and their most appropriate speed. Our task is to find our own path within ourselves and not to try to push others onto it, but to let them be true to their own. "To thine own Self be true." True charity often requires leaving another person alone. What folly and falseness and van-

The highest awareness of the mystic is expressed
by the Bodhisattva who
(in Mahayana Buddhism)
is the one who awares the Godhead
in every place, in every person, and in every thing—
and thus no longer has to retire into solitude and trance
in order to aware God.
The Bodhisattva's mystic, intuitive awareness is
identical with whatever is happening at the moment;
there is the *innerstanding* that
really and fundamentally,
all is well.

ity in our assertiveness and our Trying to share. What an imposition! What conceit of agency! Such "giving" is often nothing more than clever ego-strutting in *shakti-business*, in vain exhibitionism, and in pushy-ideal antics!

In childhood days, I had no words for my awareness. There was no urge to express and therefore no language. In looking back, things seem to have been vague, yet there were deeply rooted tendrils of feeling and of being. How good to have no "concern" either to assert or to share. Without efforting,[11] I experienced the interdependence of all beings. There was easy healing and harmonious breathing in a love that received in giving and gave in receiving. In this childhood mode of experiencing, God was the Self revealed in all things. Beyond the veil of words, there was an un-mental Awareness of true relationship and right interdependence. And in that living Awareness, there was no enthusing, no trying, no praying, no ideal beauty. Life was all too real for ecstasy and for rapture, too simple for intensity and for wonder, too rich for tears or for laughter, too deep for thought.

How do we know one another spiritually or even psychically, beyond name and shape? Egos reveal or betray themselves by their efforting, and their antics cease to satisfy. Anyway, it is not possible for egos to share in unitive awareness. Efforting and wordiness pertain to ego-consciousness. Books at best are the no longer inhabited shells of wisdom, but more often they are the exhibition-tombs of ego-consciousness. They may be interesting records of stutterings on the way, but are rarely relevant to the deeper experience of simple, living Awareness in which the soul is without words in naked alone-

"In the beginning was the Word,
and the Word was with God,
and the Word was God."

The Word was Emmanuel—
the indwelling Christ, the Logos, the Sophia.
(Notice how many of the prophets and archangels
have "**el**" in their name.)
"**Elya, Elya,** how thou hast glorified me!"

This is often translated
(in a way that is so out of keeping
with the spirit of Jesus)
as:
"My God, My God, why hast thou forsaken me."

Similarly, when Jesus later says:
"Consumatum est,"
this is often translated as the very tame statement:
"It is finished."

It should be translated as a statement of joy—
Jesus has realized
that his task has ended and
that He has accepted the Will.

(Biblical quotations
are from
John 1:1,
Matthew 27:46,
Mark 15:34, and
John 19:30)

ness. Among books, the most satisfying is the mystic book of Nature that enfolds us, and each of us at birth is presented with a unique copy of this sacred flesh-bound volume.

If one is aware of the real communion of interfusing harmonies going on all the time within and around us, one does not go out eagerly to have the vision blurred by desire-sediments of egos, by the assertions of likes and dislikes, or by the exhibition of power complexes. If one does choose to go out among the efforting noises of egos, it may be useful for the contrast to the Silence—and also for testing oneself to find if it is possible there also to know the Silence.

In the established and balanced unitive awareness of Immanence and of Transcendence, of Presence and of Being, ego ceases to usurp. Once the world is known to be a dream, there is an awakening from the efforting of becoming. When we experience God and realize our Self—livingly—our wordiness ceases and we live at ease. "The time shall come and **now is** when ye shall worship God neither in temple nor in mountain caves, but in spirit and living truth"—meaning in the Silence of the cave within. Not worship nor wordship, but unefforting worthship, which is simple, living Awareness.

Deep within each of us is an awareness of an Origin and a Destiny, this awareness being a pure reflection of our real Being. To remain conscious of this Origin and Destiny as we make our pilgrimage through the jungles of emotionalism, the mirages of mentality, and the wilderness of civilization requires that we allow ourselves to be guided by the Light of intuition. Even when we are stumbling in the darkness—deluded by ego-consciousness—that Light ever beckons us.

The advent of Spring in our beingness comes not with éclat,
but softly, silently,
breathing life into the seeming dead,
warmth into the cold,
making the seeds sprout
and the trees put forth leaves and blooms,
bringing gladness to the heart of all.
Somehow the purpose of creation
seems to be silently fulfilled in oneself,
and one becomes—
without trying or power display—
a promise of a new dawn.
It is in the total scheme of things—
if you accept and innerstand it that way.

From the Eden of the past to the Paradise which will be, through the illusion of time, we stumble and stray, yet ever we are led by the mystic light that shines in the darkness. As we slowly learn how to loose and unfold our intuitive wings, we also gain courage in using them consciously. In the fullness of time, we re-awaken and find our Self in Eternity's Sunrise here and now. We forget to Remember, but we also Remember to forget. Ego-consciousness is Self-forgetting; the dawn of Awareness is the due Re-awakening of conscious Self-identity "in the Light that never was on land or sea,"[12] but ever is—though the Light of our Sun and all the other Star-suns doth fade and cease to be.

Stilly, purely, and wordlessly, we may be aware of our Self even in the ego-play and in the *shakti-antics*, in the Light of death and in the darkness of "what ye call life." The mystic Light is within, within all things and all changes—it is the real correspondence, the immediate effortless "rapport." The mature soul is not deceived by ego-ideals and rosy-sweet sentimentality, nor is it dismayed by power-politics or by psychic storms—it remembers to re-collect its pure *memory*.

Among fellow-pilgrims, we seem to recognize the few who have come through the veils, who have arrived, and who silently and effortlessly radiate *memory*. Even their words have the quality of Silence, the fragrance of *memory*. True clairvoyance is to see vibrationally the mystic Light radiating from all forms and functions. True clair-audience is to hear calmly the soundless voice of the Sunyata-Silence, the mystic cave of our inner realm. True death is to expose the ego-deformed consciousness to the Light of the whole consciousness, the pure Life, which we **ARE**.

73

The Word is word-free.
The boat of intuition carries you across
the choppy ocean of duality,
to the source of All.
The sea of *samsara* is awared as
the ocean of grace-filled *ananda*,
not mere happiness or fluctuating joys.
Always build from **within**, not from without;
from **intuition**, not from instinct.

—From an article written by Sunyata
published in *The Call Divine*

Mencius, the Chinese sage born a century after Socrates, held that the whole of education consists in re-capturing one's "original heart"—what we would call *memory*—through the cultivation of intuitive faculties that have previously been allowed to atrophy. But for many of our modern doctors of Education and Psychoanalysis, as well as to our power-politicians and professors of Divinity, the very word "intuition" is taboo. "There ain't no such animal." The faculty of intuition is the Cinderella of all faculties, and is mocked or ignored by rationalists, factualists, and intellectualists; so it is no wonder that it atrophies in them to the extent that they have no conscious memory of intuitive synthesis or of psychic Wholeness. Psychology is still in its infancy. Psychic awareness is ignored—or it is degraded into merely seeing ghosts and other trivial phenomena. Psychic researchers seem unaware that they themselves are psyches, and that their psychic sensibilities are far vaster in scope than either their matter awareness or their mental consciousness. Most people are even unaware of the psychic vibrations which are all around us; psychic storms are called earthquakes, droughts, famines, epidemics, and wars—and our doctors try to cure the symptoms while ignoring the cause.

Such doctors of neurosis and psychosis pry and probe into the sub-conscious and the immediate past. Cleverly do they mentalize and mess about in that sombre and tiny region of our vast storehouse of psychic memory, finding with the torch-

Reply to a question about sex:
"At one level of consciousness it reigns supreme;
at another level, it doesn't matter;
and on a third level, it doesn't exist."

—Anandamayi Ma

My consciousness has never associated itself
with this temporary body.
Before I came on this earth, Pitaji,
it was the same.
As a little girl,
it was the same.
When the family in which I was born
made arrangements to have this body married,
I was the same.
And, Pitaji, in front of you now,
I am the same.
Even after the dance of creation changes
in the Hall of Eternity,
I shall be the same.

—Anandamayi Ma
("Pitaji" means "father";
it is the way Mataji
addressed men.)

light of their sparkling intellect Oedipus complexes, psychic poisons, unhealed scars, and lies disguised as facts. Semi-deified sex is put on the throne of life and is worshipped in many disguises, but rarely in its deepest cosmic significance. To them, sublimation is the goal; but again these learned ones seem to be scenting and pursuing the wrong track—sublimate what? and who is the one who sublimates? It is all very sub-lime and divine, but why not face the source, find it, and from there see the symptoms wholly? In the Light of psychic Wholeness and integral Being, our diseases may be at least accepted—and often they can be healed. The trouble is not sex, but its abuse through intellectualization: the busy-ness of sex-on-the-mind. The cause of our ignorance, fever, and fret is the psyche, which egos mock and doctors in their learned igno-rance ignore or fear. The diagnosis of psycho-analysts often seems very infantile, and where are the psycho-synthesists who are able to diagnose and cure humankind's diseases? First, we must be "saved" by becoming livingly aware of our own vast psyche, and only then can we begin to diagnose and "save" our fellow pilgrims.

The idea, and much less the truth of a super-conscious realm to our Being, is not accepted by most Western schools of Psychology. To them, the mystic realization of Life through Self-awareness is seen as a lower and more primitive state of consciousness. It must of necessity be so to mental humans until they are free from their learned inhibitions and can begin to experience life livingly and wholly.

Flashes of intuition are common among artists, geniuses, intellectuals, and women; such flashes, like lightning on a dark

Life is *ji ji muge*—
perfect, mutual, unimpeded interpenetration
and
joyous ease
in the divine Self-interplay.

To know God is to be God.

night, often flicker and become unsteady, and therefore don't lead the person to integral Being or ego-Transcendence. Similarly, although the psychic visions of ordinary seer-ship and mediumship are often mixed up with intuition and even with mysticism, the awareness is rarely ego-free. The clear, steady, and simple light of intuition is not so easily attained— for how can we acquire what is here and ours all the time? Only when we are still can it be awared. When we have slept long enough, the moment will come when we simply awake into awareness. "Ripeness is all."[13]

The *tantric* gate to psychic sensibilities is broad and easy to unlock, but the path beyond this gate has many pitfalls, especially to clever folks who think that they can play with the devil and be immune. In positive passivity, in *negative capability*, and in a purely receptive and accepting attitude, intuition grows in grace as a trustworthy tool, a key to awareness. Once intuition predominates, then the critical, analytical, and mental tools may come to its support—or at least no longer block its development.

It has been said that "Reason's extremity is Intuition's opportunity," but this seems more true of the flashy kind of intuition, and not the simple, steady Light of the mature soul. Usurping intellect does seem to bar and hinder our awareness of intuition as the leading light; once the intellect breaks and the mind is transcended, intuition may shine forth and take the lead, but this is rarely so unless the soul is mature and sure in both pose and balance. More often "Reason's extremity" brings forth muddled and confused madness. After all, there is some method to the madness of natural, simple mystics who

There is no important event for a *jnani*—
except when a fellow-being
in intuitive apperception
awakens into the grace of the Ghostly Whole—
only then his heart rejoices.
All else is of no concern.

—With respects to Nisargadatta Maharaj
I Am That,
dialogue 41

Your own Self-realization
is
the greatest form of service
you can render.

However much a *jnani* might work,
he is still the Quiet one.
However much he might talk,
he is still the Silent one.

—Ramana Maharshi

can calmly, clearly, and sagely escape the bondage of mind and be free of space and time; they do this not through abandoning their reason, but by harmonizing all of their tools to develop a simple poise.

Reason is a useful bridge between instinct and intuition, and few pilgrims can dispose of it until they know how to use their intuitive wings. If need be, let us keep our reason, but still we need not cling to it. Faith—like reason—must also be left behind. When we know livingly, we no longer need to believe in anything. When we experience God, we are silent and still, cured of our fret, our fear, and our efforting. We are at ease in life, and the search for love is left behind. The less of creature-awareness, the more of God-awareness; the more we lose our ego, the more we realize that who we are is God. He to whom the Eternal Word speaketh is set free from the multitude of opinions—that which he had lost sight of in wordiness, he may find in Solitude and in Silence.

According to a Chinese legend, it was not knowledge nor sight nor speech that could find the lost pearl of great price for the Emperor—for they but served to hide it. Once he was able to cease efforting and give up his search, he recovered the awareness of the pearl—the secret of his success was active non-striving. It had never been lost, but it was only his veil of learned ignorance that had concealed it. Similarly, this pearl is well hidden within each of us. Just as there are cosmic radiations which pass silently and unimpeded through lead, so does the unity of all Being go unaware in the world of reason. Beyond union there is unity, beyond the One is the Nought of Sunyata. Awareness is all. "Lift a stone and thou shalt find

81

An *avatar* is only a part-manifestation—
while a *jnani* is the whole.

—Ramana Maharshi

In reply to the pleadings of his mother
that he should return home,
Ramana Maharshi wrote:
"The ordainer controls the fate of beings
in accordance with
their *prarabdha karma*.
Whatever is destined not to happen will not happen,
try as you may.
Whatever is destined to happen will happen,
do what you may to prevent it—
this is certain.
The best course, therefore, is to remain Silent."

Do not fuss or worry about what you have to do or not to do.
What as work has to be done through you,
will be done whether you like it or not.
Simply be Still, be inwardly Still.

—Ramana Maharshi

82

Two years old; Århus, Denmark (1892)

On his sister's verandah with his parents, Århus (1919)

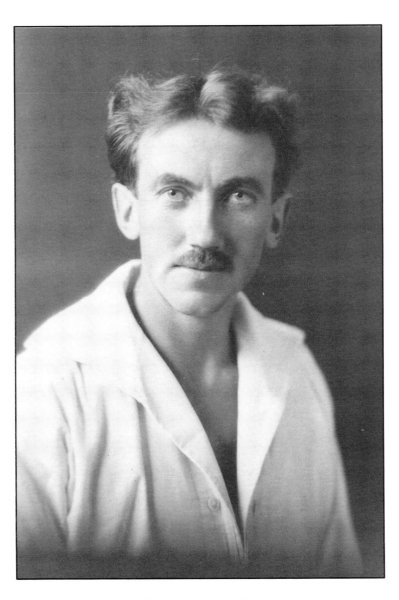

In England in the 1920's

In England (1928)

In India in the 1930's

With Wuti

In Almora, India (1959)

In India

With Lama Govinda in Almora, India

Ramana
Maharshi

In India

In Almora, India (1973)

xiii

© 1982 by Raymond Baltar

Mill Valley, California (1982)

In Chicago, 1980's

© 1984 by Olof Söderbäck

Last photograph taken of Sunyata; Fairfax, California.

Me, cleave the wood and there I am."[14] Nay, be still and experience that thou art God.

To the myopic sight of Western consciousness, one tiny part of the spectrum is visible and reigns supreme. As some individuals have told us about their giddy excursions into the unconscious above and below, we have extended the spectrum, but only slightly. As a culture, we may be dimly aware of the sub- and super-conscious strata of our psychic being, but for most individuals, the extensions are still rather small and have never been directly experienced. Instruments have made us aware of the infra-red and the ultra-violet rays invisible to the naked eye; but who will reveal to us the full vastness of the spectrum of consciousness? We will receive a wider more inclusive Light only if we open ourselves to the vaster views of a vaster Silence. Through Self-identification, we can know vibrationally of a realm where all that is (or ever has been or ever will be) is One and Whole.

There are electro-magnetic radiations and queer cosmic rays, X-rays and why-rays, which aren't even noticed as they pass through the complex brain of a blinkered scientist. While egos do find it humbling to probe the sub-conscious realms of our psyche, they are often humiliated when they begin exploring the super-mental realms. The cosmic rays of ego-free awareness may have queer effects on intellectuals; only when they go happily out of their smart minds will they be able to give up their blinkers.

The Light of intuition reveals psycho-synthesis; such a unitive mode of experiencing is the preventative and cure for both ego-antics and psychosis. Willy Shakespeare knew livingly

If any of you are satisfied with anything less
than the Experience of or in God,
you are satisfied with too little.
Nothing should satisfy you but the Experience itSelf.
Turn within, and be guided
by Ramana Maharshi's oft-repeated advice:
"Simply be Still, be inwardly Still."
Be still, but do not **try** to be
the Stillness, the Silence, and the Self-radiance
that you ever Are.

Worry not about what ye shall say or do
in the *Swa-lila* Self-interplay.
Prarabdha karma will fulfill itSelf
in and through you
no matter what you may will.
The Holy Ghost—or Ghostly Whole—
will
inform,
illuminate,
and guide you,
as it did overshadow
the (virgin) Mother
of
the Christ-conscious Joshua ben Joseph.

There's a divinity that shapes our ends,
Rough-hew them though we may.

—With respects to Shakespeare
Hamlet V, ii, 10

84

that "reason was the helper, reason is the bar":[15]

Reason, in itself confounded,
Saw division grow together . . .
Hearts remote, yet not asunder;
Distance, and no space was seen . . .
Love hath reason, reason none . . .[16]

"Reason is the bar"—but so is anything that we cling to unduly:

He who binds to himself a joy
Does the wingèd life destroy;
But he who kisses the joy as it flies
Lives in Eternity's Sunrise.[17]

Ego-memory is not truth, but persistence, a perpetuation of a transitory moment through the lie that any moment can be made permanent:

The One remains, the many change and pass;
Heaven's light forever shines, Earth's shadows fly;
Ego-life, like a dome of many-colored glass,
Stains the white radiance of Eternity,
Until Death tramples it to fragments.—Die,
If thou wouldst be with that which thou dost seek!
Follow where all is fled![18]

It is the "many-colored glass" of prejudices and emotionality that keeps us trapped in ego-memories. But if "the play's the thing,"[19] the Real is the no-thing-ness, within and beyond the changing forms and functions of the Life-*lila*.

It is through awaring the intuitive mode of consciousness

Our birth is but a sleep and a forgetting.
We seem to forget our Self,
our Divinity,
our essential Reality,
in ego-fuss and duality-antics.
When the indwelling *Emmanuel* is dormant,
we forget our Home in the invisible Real.

—With respects to Wordsworth
Intimations of Immortality,
stanza 5

and gleams of unitive *memory* that Wordsworth could know:

> Our birth is but a sleep and a forgetting:
> The Soul that rises with us, our life's Star,
>> Hath had elsewhere its setting,
>> And cometh from afar:
> Not in entire forgetfulness,
> And not in utter nakedness,
> But trailing clouds of glory do we come
> From God, who is our home:
> Heaven lies about us in our infancy!
> Shades of the prison-house begin to close
>> Upon the growing Boy
>> But he
> Beholds the light, and whence it flows,
>> He sees it in his joy; . . . .
> At length the Man perceives it die away,
> And fade into the light of common day.[20]

The Heaven that "lies about us in our infancy" is ever about us and within us. It is only an usurping ego-consciousness that has dulled our awareness of this realm. Blinkers and shutters of false Self-identification make dim to the ego the Light that ever is pristine and present. "Shades of the prison-house begin to close" and "the trailing clouds of glory . . . fade into the light of common day." We identify our Self with the ever-changing shadows of the actual and the factual world and with our physical bodies that will one day die. God is externalized and the psyche goes in search of her lost Wholeness. When the ego struts "I! I! I!" the only power that can dissolve the ego-delusions and give re-birth into Awareness is a mystic death. Our birth into ego-life—"what ye call Life"—is "but a sleep and

The Self,
the sole Reality,
alone
exists
eternally.

Tat twam asi
("That art thou" or "Thou art that")

There is only That.

The subtle essence which is the Self
of this entire world,
That is the Real,
That is the Self,
Tat twam asi.

—*Chhandogya Upanishad* 6.8.7

88

a forgetting," a death of Self-awareness. Some shadow fragments in the dream of human life now shade the pure consciousness into hues of joys and woes, of intensity and weariness, of likes and dislikes:

> Our noisy years seem moments in the being
> Of the eternal Silence . . .
> Hence in a season of calm weather
> Though inland far we be,
> Our souls have sight of that immortal sea
> Which brought us hither . . ."[21]

We are "that immortal sea."

The soul has *memory* and our intuition will dissolve the shadows of mind and the sediments of desires. Truth is within ourselves. Whatever an ego may believe, the truth can never have its source in outward things; useless is the effort to make an entry for a light supposed to be without. There is an innermost center in us all, where truth abides in fullness, and to "know" consists in opening an exit so that this imprisoned splendor can escape.

Poets, geniuses, and artists often have gleams of *memory*, but yet their awareness is often fleeting, unbalanced, and uncoordinated with the Whole. It is only the sages and mystics who become that *memory*, and thus are consciously, calmly, and clearly aware of Being their Self, and thus forever free both of the disease of becoming and the urge to assert and explain.

"In the whole world,
there is nothing but God."

—Shouted to Sunyata by a Bengali youth
chopping onions inside a little shop
in a Calcutta slum

Serenely they radiate—free from ideals, enthusing, and efforting; they are rid of the duty-complex, fear, and hope. Expectation is in itself bondage, and neither vivid intensity nor showy vitality are modes of wisdom or of awareness. In our timeless moments of Eternity, we simply ARE—still and aware—beyond both wisdom and ignorance. The sleeping, dreaming, and waking states are but modes passing before the Self; as egos, "we are such stuff as dreams are made of, and our little life is rounded with a sleep"[22]—the healing "sleep" that we call death.

All the mystic poets in all ages have stuttered their intimation of *memory*, and in gleams of Self-Awareness, their thought, though ego-born, became winged and fragrant with *memory*. But though their art was the helper, art often became the bar; the search for facile expressions and trained tricks would often become a new bondage.

Wordsworth speaks of *memory* when he writes:

In such access of mind, in such high hour
Of visitation from the living God,
Thought was not; in enjoyment it expired.
No thanks he breathed, he proffered no request;
Rapt into still communion that transcends
The imperfect offices of prayer and praise.[23]

But elsewhere Wordsworth is very wordy, and ever trying to recapture *memory*. He often seems to be trying laboriously to go beyond thought, beyond rapture, beyond ego-consciousness, and to be where Being is free and efforts are stilled.

The Whole does not enthuse. In the unitive mode of expe-

When the Basrah Sufi awoke Self-illumined,
he ran about shouting:
"Anur Huk! Anur Huk!"
("I am God! I am God!")
The word symbols were unfortunate and
the shouting was immature.
So, naturally, our Sufiji had his godly head chopped off
by the fanatic orthodox brethren.
Why shout or assert?
Better to keep mum and God-free
and
live It
with joyous ease,
affectionate detachment, and
delightful uncertainty.

riencing, there is a sense of completion, of unbroken perfection, and of achievement without doing. To a mind that is still, the whole universe surrenders—simply, untryingly, livingly. We can reflect and know our Self as more than all these Universes.

Percy Shelley "shrieked in ecstasy" and so do many emotional saints and sickly geniuses. In mystic visitations, Friends do quake and novices agitate. It is an error to try to tell others about our mystic experiences—and even worse to be solemn about them by giving long-winded muddled explanations; wise is the person who follows Blake's warning:

Never seek to tell thy love
Love that never told can be;
For the gentle wind does move
Silently, invisibly.

I told my love, I told my love,
I told her all my heart;
Trembling, cold, in ghastly fears —
Ah, she doth depart.[24]

Similarly, our deepest joy, our richest awareness is too real for telling, for tears, or even for thought. It never can be told in words, nor conveyed to anybody who does not already know it livingly. Trying to tell about it may help to clarify the experience to one's own self (one's ego), but it will shortly become apparent how it is impossible to explain what happened to others. What have other egos and intellects to do with it? They only wriggle and twist thoughts, for they do not like to die, to be expunged, to be mutated, or to be exposed to the invisible Sun of Being, the invisible Reality which is glibly called "God." Better to have no need to clarify the illu-

Intuition has much more to do with feeling
than with thinking.
Intuitive feelings of harmony, of unity, and
of love . . . everywhere, radiant.
Thinking is always dualistic.
Something has to think of something else.
That's why I like Shakespeare's line:
"There is nothing either good or bad
but thinking makes it so."
So get beyond thinking, beyond thought.
And that you can do in meditation, in Silence.

To God, all is beautiful, good, and as it should be.
Humans must see things as either good or bad.

—Herakleitos
Fragment 106

All is right that seems most wrong (to clever egojies).

sory intellect and the equally illusory ego, better to have no urge to understand what has been experienced livingly—and better to heal our dis-ease of wordiness and Be what we Are. We can tell our truth in the language which seems to be Silence because it is full beyond words. The mystic Life-Awareness will tell itself effortlessly. Our trying is fatal, futile, and blurring. Silence intuits and many pilgrims know and share in this eloquent language. One is never lonely or lonesome when one is alone in all Oneness.

John Keats may "tease us out of thought as doth Eternity"[25] and Willy Shakespeare may confirm that "there is nothing either good or bad but thinking makes it so."[26] But how few have consciously, steadily, and calmly been aware of Eternity in the here and now? How few have had a glimpse of being free of time, thought, and desire—thereby experiencing directly the Living Silence of Being? Until that moment, they can only have a stunted and truncated vision of their Self. How few have solved the paradox—or antinomy—of immanence and transcendence through the direct experience of mystic consummation. "Thought was not" and "there shall be no more time"—what do such phrases and "poetic lies" convey to fellow-pilgrims, who have not consciously been their Self beyond thought, beyond time, and beyond efforting? Is ego-transcendence the goal? Do we know it experientially, or do we merely profess its virtues?

Out of one's thought, out of one's mind, out of the bonds of time and space, yet including these: it must appear to be a demented state of affairs, a vacuum, a cessation of all that seems good and sensible to egos, though they themselves do

In and with all your imperfections,
YOU are perfect.

Let Life flow on its own—
let the current lead you.
Be like a white cloud in the Krishna-blue sky,
like *akasha*:
no goal,
no power,
no will,
going nowhere, just floating.
That flowing is ultimate flowering.
Everything unnatural has to be avoided.
Be natural.
Self-nature is enough, you cannot improve upon it.

queer things in order to "pass away the time." But where can "time" be passed? And where are we ourselves off to in the procession of assertively strutting egos:

> But man, proud man,
> Drest in a little brief authority,
> Most ignorant of what he's most assured,
> His glassy essence, like an angry ape,
> Plays such fantastic tricks before high heaven
> As make the angels weep.[27]

More likely, the angels are laughing.

Men say, "Time passes"; Time says, "Men pass." Whence? Whither? Aye, all illusions pass. Whither are we all progressing in such a vital hurry. What are egos becoming? Superegos? Can they transcend ego-consciousness into awareness? If we are sincere pilgrims of Eternity with queer mystic urges and strange *memory*, why not enter the awareness of the Eternal now, immediately, this very moment? As William Blake pointed out, it is all so simple . . .

> To see a world in a grain of sand
> And a heaven in a wild flower,
> Hold infinity in the palm of your hand
> And eternity in an hour.[28]

Without desire, it is possible to still the streams of thought, the waves of the mind. Then enter effortlessly and harmoniously—free of qualities or ego-hues, without masks or disguises—into the radiant dark Light of Wholeness, of living Ease, of rich Silence. In the steady light of our intuition, we can move lightly and learn to freely wing our way. We can go

Once you realize and experience that the world
is your own projection,
you are free of it (and in it).

The real "I" is always here—
it never appears or disappears.
The error and the bondage is the feeling that
"I am the body" or "the body is I"—
the false sense of "I" must go.

beyond ego-delusions and diseased tools—once we know livingly and simply that they are not who we are. All in the fullness of time, now and here.

In the willful, intellectual, and emotional approaches to mystic experience, the ecstatic shrieks and vital enthusings are likely to occur and to re-occur. The vivid sights and sudden rendings of the veils can be viewed as signs from heaven, wondrous miracles, or "*siddhi* tricks." All these phenomena, though indicative, are not in themselves very important; such a *darshan*—although so extra-ordinary—is usually fleeting or dim because of the desires that still remain. Rarely do shrieks or groans of ecstasy occur in the passive clarification of either natural contemplation or simple mystic consummation. What is most conducive to the simple, calm dissolving of the veils is the effortless stilling of both mind and desire. The "miracles" of the promised land need not evoke rhapsodies when what is experienced is the gradual, natural, and unsensational unfolding of what Is.

In this simple, effortless, and living acceptance, there is no exaltation, but a calm, joyous awareness of becoming and begoing, of the rising and ceasing of all things, or, rather, of the Life which we Are, bubbling playfully through its myriad forms. It becomes harmoniously easy to make the shift in consciousness away from the details of the moment to dwell in Eternity; similarly, when we return to that which we call actual and factual—in contrast to the True and the Real—there is hardly any effort or choice in this outward journey. No regret, and no wish to hold or to have. The Light is One there as it is here. We learn not to cling either to things or to ego-mem-

There is nothing to forgive and no forgiver.
Thou art thy Self the object of thy search.

The meanest flea
as it is in God
is superior to the highest angel
as he is in himself.

—Meister Eckhart,
13th century German mystic

The Light that leadeth astray
is
also light from Heaven.

There is no death of the Real.

ories, and dying becomes easy. *Memory* remains, and, in the fullness of time, we learn to make a good death.

As we mature and our wings of intuition grow stronger, the shifts in consciousness become easier and more natural. For those who have learned to shed ego-consciousness, there is no need for rigid trances or even for solitude. Solitude is within, and the Real is the most natural. The actual, the factual, and even ego-antics are also modes of the Real and can be seen as true, right, and inevitable on their own level and in their own time and place. Everything is part of the endless, unbroken perfection. Once everything is accepted livingly, all is forgiven—and there is nothing to forgive, nothing to regret.

When we experience livingly that there is no detachment from what is Real, there can no longer be any bonds of attachment or any fear of what is unfamiliar and unknown. The soul is freely at Home in the One Life, aware on various levels of the different modes of experiencing, but just as at Home in ego-noises as in the mystic Silence.

There are many shapes of mystery, and all are good, even the devil. In the mode of unitive experiencing, we accept the various emphases and the changing hues, we accept them livingly as our Self at play. Death is also part of Life, so why fuss and flutter? Why joy at arrival and then grieve at departure? Why shriek in joy and then shrink in fear? Only children who have ceased to be child-like and fellow-pilgrims who have forgotten *memory* must flutter in mental attachments by collecting memories. We can know livingly. We always have *memory* —our pre-natal natural Wisdom—and this can be recollected at any time. This autobiographical ego-scribble is simply a fra-

Remember your original face—
the one you had before you were born.

grance of my childhood's *memory* put into a muddle of words, a dis-ease of wordiness and of explaining.

In the rich solitude of my childhood, Life seemed a moving prayer, and so there was neither urge nor occasion for spoken prayer and praise. What was there to pray for? Who was there to be praised or worshipped in words? In childhood, I did not suffer from the dis-ease of wordiness. I did not dissipate. It is only necessary to communicate to one another when there is a sense of duality. Only as egos do we desire to support, to lean on, or to explain to one another in wordy nearness and in the illusion of sharing.

Deep contemplation is Eternal speech, while Silence is unceasing eloquence—speaking can only interrupt this language of the Real. To the soul whose inner ear is attuned to the soundless Voice in the Silence, our wordy prayers for something or for somebody are not Real enough. They pertain to the immature consciousness, to the blinkered state of duality. In the state of prayerfulness, all is well. Below the surface waves and the foam-flecks of beautiful differences is the unefforted harmony of unifying "rapport." Measure not in words the immeasurable—sink not the string of thoughts into the fathomless. There is no chart for what is most enduring. Thoughts break, intellect is transcended, and lo!—Reality is again aware of Itself. When the trickle of thoughts stops agitating the mind, the mind becomes like a clear and calm lake—it is ready to reflect the Word, the alone begotten Sun of Silence.

Why try to make muddy water clear? Leave it alone, and by itself, it will soon clarify and reflect the Sun and the starry heavens. The living intuitive Wisdom, or direct experience of

The natural property of a wing
is
to raise
that which is heavy
and
carry it aloft
to the region where the gods dwell . . .

—Socrates
Plato's *Phaedrus* 246E

Reality, is independent of symbols, thought, sensation, learning, education, position, or any of life's circumstances. When we transcend the questioning mind and our conceit of agency, we will then be open to the Breath of Heaven—the mighty voice of the Silence within—and even to know our identity with the universal cosmic Self.

The mature ego grows calm and clear, and by itself—once still—dissolves. If the intellect says "yes" to this annihilation, the spirit will then travel free. However, if the silly clever intellect wants to continually puzzle over whether this or that is—or is not—planned, it is then placing weights on that person's intuitive wings. What can the intellect know of things beyond itself? Its failures and its successes can only suggest and indicate that living Beyondness, which is also within, and when it has finished suggesting, it may be quiet, like a good and well used tool.

When Life itself is lived in a state of prayerfulness, there is no need of prayers. When one is intimately familiar with the book of Nature, there is no need of words. Then each individual can be aware of his or her own flesh-bound volume. Balanced introspection and extrospection, going in and going out, in calm harmonious poise, lead to awareness of the microcosm within, and in that awareness—lo! life is an open book, and they who are awake may read livingly.

When troubles and problems and choices assailed me as a child, I nearly always instinctively went within and contemplated them from there. In Solitude and in Silence, the child instinctively sought *memory*, and usually, in its mystic-clear light, the pains and the problems were healed—or at least

Don't search for anyone's blessing.
No human can be the real Guru.
All blessings come from within—or from beyond.
Thou art thy Self the object of thy search

Submission to the *Sadguru* is
not submission to anyone outside of one's Self,
but this Self is manifested outwardly
in order to help one
to discover the Self within:
the seeming two are one—the Master is within.

Effort was the helper—effort is the bar.
Reason was the helper—reason is the bar.
Ego was the helper—ego is the bar.
Guru was the helper—**guru** is the bar.

Egojies think they create, evolve, and
experience re-volutions.
They think that they push and pull,
achieve and attain,
conquer and control—
but all the eternal while,
they are being pushed and pulled,
used and guided.
There is sure guidance by an inner *bhagavan*,
who pulls the string,
who speaks in Silence, and
enjoys itSelf in the puppet dream.

accepted. In regard to my deepest problems and in search for
true direction, I did not seek outside advice, sympathy, or love.
Slowly or quickly, some kind of answers were always forth-
coming to my whither? my how? and my why? and by trial
and error, by testing and by success, I learned to move and to
act in the Light of intuition. I came to find the guidance of the
inner Guru less confusing than the advice, the suggestions, and
the explanations of fellow-pilgrims. In regard to my own steps
on the *Tao*, I may have gone slower—even stumbled and fell,
gotten hurt and scarred—but I learned by my own mistakes
how not to repeat them. I learned my weaknesses and my
strengths, and through walking alone, the peace became part of
my own natural rhythm and momentum, simple and unforced.

It is true that extroverted children may need an outer
Guru, but always that which re-cognizes the Guru and the
guidance as true comes from within ourSelf; in the fullness
of time, each disciple comes to realize that the real Guru—
like the real Kingdom of the Self—is ever within. It is easy
to be a Guru—there are many. The Life in everything may be
our Guru—the most simple form may reveal itSelf to us, and
they who have one end in view will make all things serve. It
is the re-cognition we lack, the insight, the single, naked sincerity of Being—and so it is that there are but few real *chelas*
or "disciples." Many like to pass as "disciples," but few like
to be "disciples." Ego is in the way. False self-identification
blocks our going, but we are all on the way, and as we become
more mature, so we increase our flair for maintaining our
balance and seeing our direction. In the Light of intuition,
the illusory ego dissolves and *Swa-raj*—Self-rule—Is. It is a

You may pray for your needs,
but not for your wants, whims, and predilections.
Want is the duality of the future.
Don't want.
Just Be.

When I pray for aught, my prayer goes for naught.
When I pray for something, I pray at my weakest.
When I pray for nothing, I pray at my strongest.
And when I want nothing and make no request,
I AM praying at my best.

What you need will come to you—
if you refrain from asking for what you don't need.

—Sri Nisargadatta Maharaj

All is well—
all is righteous—
and marvelously beautiful and lovable as IT IS.
Why ask that it may be different?
Why even pray that "Thy Will be done"—
The Will is ever being done in the divine *Swa-lila*.
Rejoice in gratitude—
and endure patiently what you cannot enjoy.

matter of awakening rather than conquest. **"Guru** *was* the helper—**guru** *is* the bar."

During the intermediate period, between the bodily ages of 7 and 14, when ego and mind usurped the place of intuition, I recall only two instances of having prayed—officially, sincerely, and orally—to a God in some vague "heaven" outside of myself. These two fits of prayer occurred at the bodily age of 12 and each was a response to a crisis.

The first occurred during summertime. Then, when all the cows of Viking land are let into the fertile fields, they are tied by ropes; the peg to which the rope is tied is then "advanced" 4 or 5 times in the course of each day so as to allow the cows more grass. One day, in an urge of freedom, one of our cows got loose and managed to get to the clover fields where she gobbled up a great amount of the forbidden herb. Fermentation set in and caused acute tension and a war of expansion in Daisy's tummy, and very quickly she was dying. Like the little *Nisse* in the Andersen fairytale, who in a crisis knew that to him the tattered poetry-book was more real than the grocer and his porridge,[29] I also knew my values. Quickly I ran into the empty stable where I could be alone to pray fervently (and almost loudly) to God that the agonized cow might live. She was my intimate friend, and also we could ill-afford to lose her. I thought my most essential help was to bring Daisy's plight to the attention of the Almighty, who could easily save us all from this calamity. However, I soon realized God thought otherwise

A great sadhu in India had cancer and wrote me
(before he gave his body to an operation
that he knew was to be fatal):
"All is right that seems most wrong."

You who wish to celebrate a birthday,
seek first—whence was your birth?
One's true birth is when one enters THAT—
which transcends birth and death—
the Eternal Being.
At least on one's birthday one should mourn
one's entry into the realm of *samsara*.
To glory in it and to celebrate is like
delighting in and decorating a corpse.
To seek one's Self and merge in It—
this is Wisdom.

—Ramana Maharshi

Your highest glory and grace is where you cease to exist.

—Ramana Maharshi

Ego-oblivion is Self-awareness.

(when I found Daisy dead); I also got a sound scolding from my mother for having absented myself, "gallivanting" instead of "helping." The grown-up children had preached at me: "Ask and it shall be given unto you"—but they had not emphasized that the Perfect Father is kind of neutral in war-time. I was disappointed in "Him."

I must have forgiven God, for shortly afterwards I tried "Him" again in all sincerity, when a boy who for some years had been my dear companion on the farm, chose to go back to his own family in the city. In the privacy of the smelly chicken-house, I secretly and vehemently implored God that Karl might not want to go. But the Lord of Hosts seemed to be a failure. "He" proved to be sublimely indifferent to the whims and moods and cravings of my ego—and so I gave up my short-lived external image of an exoteric God, and turned instead to Henrik Ibsen.

At that time, the subjective child had begun to feel puzzled by the sentimental weakness and seeming insincerity among my talkative fellow-pilgrims who called themselves "believers" and "professors." It now seems that the awakening intolerance and the exercise of critical, analytical faculties were partly due to my mis-conception of the term "faith," which to most of the good folks around me must have meant something external—like an overcoat or an ideal disguise, something taught by books, preachers, and teachers—while to me it meant something living, something akin to Wisdom: an almost doubtless conviction, which was simply lived and which conditioned our actions, attitudes, and relationships. That their faith or truth were not mine did not matter; I was indignant that they were not true to their own Light and their

At every moment,
whatever happens is for the best;
it may appear painful and ugly,
a suffering bitter and meaningless,
yet considering the past and the future,
it is for the best—
as the only way out of a disastrous situation.

—Sri Nisargadatta Maharaj
I Am That,
dialogue 98

When you are no longer attached to anything,
you have done your share.
The rest will be done for you.

What Paul says about Peter tells us more about Paul
than about Peter.
All our destructive criticism,
accusations,
and malignant charges of others
are our ego-projections;
that which focuses on and re-cognizes
these supposed blemishes
is within ourselves.
The sun has spots,
and these are a part of its Wholeness and Self-radiance.

wordy "professions," and I felt impatient at the divergence between "faith" and the actual and factual daily doings of the faithful. The believers seemed make-believers; these insincere theorists and talkers became so tiresome to me because whenever I believed their words, I would be consistently let down by their deeds. And so the Viking-child waxed resentfully and reacted in righteous wrath.

On their various changing levels of consciousness, the good folks were no doubt true to the moment and to its moods, but the mind which just then grew on me was more single, more central, or perhaps only more blinkered. It began to judge and to condemn. It responded to the battle-cry: "Nought or All." If "God" was the truth of our Being, how could we make any compromises in essential truths? I demanded of others that they be wholly and fully who they were—without pretty disguises or insincere poses. So the child memorized Henrik's challenge and recited it to the Silence:

Soul, be faithful unto the last;
The victory of victories is to lose everything.
The loss of all constitutes your winning.
Eternally you possess (or are) only that which
you have lost.[30]

Fancy this solemn Viking-boy at the "mature" age of 13 responding to such a paradoxical victory through death and loss. But there was a certain recognition of inner levels of consciousness and of Self-identification beyond that of ego. I felt that if I really believed livingly in "God" and that it was true that all was "His"—all is "He"—I must live, talk, and be silent

When you are free from desire and fear,
you will live a life so different
from all you know,
so much more interesting and intense,
that, truly,
by losing all, you gain all.

—With respects to Sri Nisargadatta Maharaj
I Am That,
dialogue 97

A level of mental maturity is reached
when nothing external
is of any value
and the heart is ready to relinquish all.

—Sri Nisargadatta Maharaj
I Am That,
dialogue 98

When the ancient Masters said,
"If you want to be given everything,
give everything up,"
they weren't using empty phrases.
Only in being lived by the *Tao*
can you be truly yourself.

—Lao-tzu
Tao Te Ching,
Chapter 22

accordingly. I wanted to be free of poetic and sentimental lies. I saw that words, if they were not kept or were not true, became a power for evil, a kind of living lie in the soul hindering the harmonious Awareness and ease of Being.

Ego-desires, outer possessions, power complexes, agonizing sufferings, and even bodily death were nought compared with the Reality of living an immanent Life—in which we shared with God a Whole Eternity. What did the brief agonies and crucifixions of saints and martyrs signify in comparison? What did Job's slow trials in time matter in the Light of Eternity? Is not the Spirit real? Is not Eternity more real than time and changing bodies? Emmanuel took large views, and he needed a few crucifixions to cure his solemnity and make him accept livingly and without judgment the fear-laden blinkers, the make-believe ideals, and the image-making love of fellow-pilgrims.

Memory had faded and the prison house of mind and of ego-consciousness was fast closing upon the growing boy. However, there was still an aroma of *memory*; unprompted by any fellow-beings or any outer force, he hailed the ego-surrender or ego-transcendence in mystic death as it was depicted in Henrik Ibsen's dramas *Brand* and *When We Dead Awaken*.

After I first heard about Henrik's stirring and controversial plays—they were brought to my notice through the daily or weekly journals—I wanted to find out more about what he had to say. Parents and people around me were all anti-Ibsen, but quietly I went to a second-hand shop in the city where I traded my boots and other odd "essentials" for an unbound *Collected Works of Henrik Ibsen*, a marvelous exchange. There was much scolding and frightening opposition from the angry wordy

I know what you are trying to do,
but you forget that I AM not what you think I am.
I do not suffer.
I cannot suffer because I AM not an object.
Of course there is suffering.
But do you realize what this suffering is?
I AM—the suffering.
Whatever is manifested,
I AM the functioning.
Whatever is perceptible,
I AM the perceiving of it.
Whatever is done,
I AM the doing of it.
And understand this:
I AM also that which is done.
In fact I AM—the total functioning.

—With respects to Nisargadatta Maharaj
Pointers from Nisargadatta Maharaj,
Chapter 56: The Last Days: Last Teaching

When asked about suffering, Sunyata would say:
"Find out who it is that suffers."

I never found the companion
that was so companionable as
solitude.
I am for the most part more lonely
when I go abroad among men
than when I stay in my chambers.

—Henry David Thoreau,
Walden
Chapter 5: Solitude

ones when they discovered me reading *Peer Gynt* and *When We Dead Awaken* written by that awfully wicked "free-thinker." They believed that thoughts, like cows, should be securely tied and should run only in fixed grooves (though not under the Pope's safe guidance), and to be a "free-thinker" was considered to be something as horrible as the devil. Henrik was seen by them as a terrible, pernicious, and poisonous influence, but Emmanuel said little, and let the storm blow over. Soon he was feeling that Henrik Ibsen was his best friend.

I remained quietly in my inner Light, seemingly unknown to any living soul, rich rather than lonely in solitude, and if I was sometimes lonely in noisy company, I would endure it patiently. "In solitude we may well find what we often lose abroad," said the writer of *The Imitation of Christ*; he also confessed: "As often as I have gone among men, I have returned home less a man."[31] But the Silence was not far off. The passive and inoffensive child made few claims, and craved but little attention, and so he was not much seen or even noticed. He was not "vital" nor "creative" in outer *shakti* busy-ness. Those around him were so busy stirring up sediments through their antics, assertions, and explanations that the child could remain hidden. Silence was the lovely veil which the word-mongers had not the time nor the patience to see through. Although the child could not have put it in these words, he saw that egos fear a Silence that might reveal a glimpse of Eternity.

The boy still laughed and wept, responded and played—life went on normally and ordinarily in the surface *lila*—but there was always that beyondness which is revealed to babes in Silence, and which must be forever veiled and

Do not forget the date of Wuji's 100th birthday party in 1990:
amidst the music of the spheres and
Wuji's drole antics,
ambrosia, amrit, and *soma juice* will be served.
Wuji makes no effort to be understood or overstood,
as he innerstands awarely—
and so he can shout:
mere knowledge is no more than
mere learned ignorance and mere happiness.

Death

Die as you are
so that you can be—
that which you really are.
Die in all your
inauthenticity, phoniness,
separation from existence.
We go on believing
that we are separate.
We are not—
not even for a single moment.
Drop the idea of separation—
and the fear of death ... .
disappears.
If you become one
with the whole,
you will live forever.
You will go beyond
birth and death.

—Bhagwan Sri Rajneesh

remain unknown to egos, to ego-consciousness, and to the intellect. The psyche has *memory* and needs no telling, no explaining. The all is Self-revealed. "Awareness is all."[32] What mania for ego-expression is the so-called "self-expression" of modern education, fostered, led, and duly colored by dictator power-politicians, white, red, green, brown, and black. How few among the shakti-players have the power of maturity—or of *memory*—to re-awaken into the ease of Being that comes with the unefforted Awareness of the ever-present Self-expression, eternally here and now?

Partly due to lingering *memory*, I quietly escaped education, or rather it did not fall upon me, and I did not reach out for it, did not seek it, and felt no urge or desire for its blessings. Likewise, later on I would "escape" property, marriage, fame, ambition, art, organization, intellect, and—in truth—all ties and attachments. Apparently, in this life, there was no need for the lessons that they have to offer.

In childhood consciousness, there was but little urge to understand what I knew intuitively and no urge to "explain" to others, to be understood, or to share ego needs, except those I had to share in. My *memory* and mode of experiencing could not be asserted, and sharing was everywhere, unblurred by efforting.

We sometimes meet—now and again—fellow-beings in a human form (though not among egos) who are kindred spirits; they reveal that they are mutely and maturely aware that sharing, knowing, and unclinging love simply Are, and do not lessen with time or distance or the death of bodies. In real rapport and in true sharing, Silence is the most real conductor, the clearest medium; but to these established few, even thoughts

You are the whole: the Ghostly Whole.
Just wake up from the dream of separateness
of being merely a human, mortal egoji.
You are the Self—the Eternal Life—
beyond birth and death and all opposites.
Thou art thy Self the object of thy search.
Ego-oblivion is Self-awareness.
Wake up—into the Ghostly Whole:
Being—Awareness—Grace: *Tat twam asi.*

—Sunyata's Last Saying,
written several weeks
before leaving his body

Lo! I AM (is) always with you, so BE—of good cheer!

—Last words of Joshua ben Joseph
(more commonly known as Jesus Christ);
with respects to *Matthew* 28:20

The rest is . . . Silence.

—The last words spoken by Hamlet,
Prince of Denmark
Hamlet V, ii, 372

and words do not blur, do not matter. Words, too, are part of the Unity and can be livingly accepted and seen through. If the Silence did not play also in these and in all discords, limitations, and noises, they would not be. Awareness is all. Vain are the thousand creeds that move men's heart, unutterably vain, in the Living Light of Awareness. Dogmas and beliefs, ideals and prejudices—all make the clarification of consciousness into awareness difficult, almost impossible. Wonder and worry, enthusing and impatience, all the muddled waves of desire must be stilled, and Life finds a way, aye, is the Way. The paradox of a transcendent yet immanent Self is reconciled in the realization that comes through a mystical experience of Unitive Awareness. Dying is the secret of mystic living.

As Dante says, in contemplation we are more than human beings; the angels of Paradise—always aware of God—have no need of memories, thoughts, or doctrines.[33] Through Silence of the senses, Silence of the imagination, Silence of the intellect, and—most important—Silence of desire and thought, the Self is both awared and Self-Aware.

In the inner Light of *memory*, we can experience our Self as pure consciousness, as more than all these Universes.

The Goblin and the Grocer:
A fairytale by Hans Christian Andersen

There was once an ordinary student: he lived in a garret, and nothing at all belonged to him; but there was also once an ordinary grocer: he lived on the ground floor, and the whole house was his: and the goblin stayed with him, for on every Christmas-eve, the grocer would leave out a bowl of rice-pudding with a great piece of butter floating on the top. The grocer was able to give that much, and so the goblin stuck to the grocer's shop, and there he learned quite a bit.

One evening the student came through the back door to buy candles and cheese for himself. He had no one to send, and that's why he came himself. He bought what he wanted and paid for it, and the grocer and his wife both nodded a "good evening" to him; and the wife was one who could do more than merely nod—she had an immense power of tongue!

And the student nodded in return, and then suddenly stood very still, reading the sheet of paper in which the cheese had been wrapped. It was a page torn out of an old book, a book that ought not to have been torn up, a book filled with poetry.

"Yonder lies some more of the same sort," said the grocer, "I gave an old woman a little coffee for that book; give me two pennies and you shall have the remainder."

"Yes," said the student, "give me the book instead of the cheese; I can eat my bread and butter without cheese. It would be a sin to tear up the rest of this book. You are a marvelous man, a practical man, but you understand no more about poetry than does that barrel in the corner."

Now, that was an insulting speech, especially toward the barrel; but the grocer laughed and the student laughed, for it was said only in jest. However, the goblin was angry that anyone should dare to say such a thing to a grocer who owned his own house and sold the best butter in town.

When night fell and the shop was closed and all were in bed, the goblin came forth and went into the bedroom, and took away the good lady's tongue, for she did not need it while she was asleep. Whenever the goblin put this tongue on any object in the room, that object acquired speech, and could express its thoughts and feelings as well as the lady herself could have done; but only one object could use it at a time, and that was a good thing, otherwise they would have all talked at the same time.

And the goblin laid the tongue on the barrel in which the old newspapers were lying.

"Is it true," the goblin asked, "that you don't know what poetry is?"

"Of course, I know poetry," replied the barrel, "poetry is something that lies at the foot of the columns in the newspaper, and is sometimes cut out. I dare swear I have more of it in me than the student, and I'm only a poor barrel compared to the grocer."

Then the goblin put the tongue on the coffee-mill, and lo!

how it began to go! And he put it on the butter-cask, and on the cash-drawer: they all shared the barrel's opinion, and the opinion of the majority must be respected.

"Oh, won't I light into that student!" thought the goblin, as he tiptoed up the back stairs to the garret where the student lived. There was still a lamp burning in his room, and when the goblin peeped through the keyhole, he saw that the student was reading the tattered old book that he had bought in the grocery shop.

But how light it was in his room! Out of the book shot a clear beam, expanding into a thick stem, and into a mighty tree, which grew upward and spread its branches far above the student. Each leaf was fresh, and every blossom had the face of a lovely young girl, some with dark sparkling eyes, others with eyes of the clearest blue; every fruit was a gleaming star, and the room resounded with the glorious sound of song.

Never had the little goblin sensed the possibility for such splendor, far less had he ever seen it. He stood still on the tips of his toes, peeping and peering until the light went out in the student's room. But even after the student blew out the lamp and went to bed, still the little goblin stayed to listen outside the door, for the music continued on, soft and beautiful—a splendid cradle song for the student who had lain down to rest.

"Nothing can be as magnificent as this," said the goblin, "I never expected such a thing! I would like to stay with this student."

And then the goblin thought it over—for he was quite a sensible and reasonable goblin too—and he sighed, "But the student has no rice-pudding to give me." So he tiptoed away, back down to the grocer's shop, and it was a very good thing that he got down there at last, for the barrel had almost worn out the good woman's tongue, for it had read out all the newspapers contained in it from top to bottom and was about to now read them out from bottom to top when the goblin came in, and restored the tongue to its rightful owner. But from then on, the whole shop, from the cash-drawer down to the firewood, took their opinions from the barrel and gave him much respect; they thought so much of him that when the grocer afterwards read the theater and art reviews in the newspaper, they were all convinced that the opinions were those of the barrel itself.

However, the little goblin could no longer sit and listen contentedly to all the wisdom down there. No! as soon as the light glimmered in the garret that evening, he felt as if the rays of light were a sturdy rope drawing him upstairs to go and peep through the keyhole; and there, a feeling of greatness possessed him, such as we might feel upon the ever-heaving sea in a raging storm when God's awesome power is rushing over us—and he burst into tears! He did not know himself why he was weeping, but there was such a blessed feeling in his crying. How wonderfully glorious it would be to sit beside the student under the same tree of light! But that could not be—so he was glad to be looking through the keyhole. There he stood in the cold hallway, with an autumn wind blowing full down upon him from the trap-door to the roof—it was cold, oh so cold, but the little fellow didn't feel it until the light in the room was long out and the song in the tree gave way to the whistle of the wind. Ugh! then he shivered, and trembled as he crept down again to his own warm corner, where it was cozy and snug.

And when Christmas came, and he saw his bowl of rice-pudding with the great lump of butter on top, why, then he remembered that the grocer was his master.

Later, in the middle of Christmas night, the goblin was awakened by a terrible tumult. People were banging noisily against the window-shutters and the watchman was blowing his horn, for a great fire had broken out and the entire street was filled with smoke and was made red by the flames. Where was the fire? Was it in his own house or at a neighbor's? Where was it? Everyone was seized by terror. The grocer's wife was in such a panic that she took her gold earrings off of her ears and put them into her pocket, just to be sure that she would save something. The grocer scurried to look for his stocks and bonds, and the maid ran for her black silk mantilla head-covering that she had scrimped and saved to buy. Each wanted to save what they treasured the most, and so did the little goblin. In a few leaps, he was up the stairs and into the room of the student, who stood quite peacefully at the open window, watching the fire that was raging in the house of the neighbor across the street. The goblin snatched the wonderful book from the table, tucked it into his red cap, and held the cap tight with both hands. The great treasure of the house was saved! And now he ran up and away—onto the roof of the house and then all the way up onto the top of the chimney. There he sat, illuminated by the flames of the house burning across the street, both hands clasping the cap which held the treasure.

Now he knew his own true feelings and to whom his heart really belonged. But when the fire was put out, and the goblin could think calmly again, then he said to himself, "I'll divide myself between the two—I can't quite give up the grocer because of his rice-pudding!"

Now, that was spoken quite like a human. We, too, must visit the grocer for our rice-pudding.

Notes

1. Socrates' term was *anamnesis*—which is usually translated as either "recollection" or "memory"; Socrates ideas about *anamnesis* are presented by Plato in the *Phaedo* (72e–77d) and *Phaedrus* (246a–250d).

2. When "blessed solitude" is "solitary beatitude," then "aloneness" is experienced as "All-One-ness."

3. Sunyata is referring to Mahatma Gandhi and the members of Gandhi's family active in the Indian independence movement. After Sunyata took Indian citizenship in 1953, Jawaharlal Nehru met him at a Danish Embassy function and told him: "Brother Alfred, Sunya-bhai, has paid us the highest compliment by becoming one of us."

4. Sunyata sometimes used "we" rather than "I" to refer to himself; in India, this usage implies that one is no longer identified with one's body, mind, or ego.

5. This concludes the new "beginning" added in California in 1980 to replace the lost pages of the original manuscript.

6. *Psalms* 139:8–10

7. *Genesis* 19:26.

8. By writing "sine-cere" in this way, Sunyata is pointing out that the word "sincere" is derived from the Latin roots meaning "without decay."

9. *The Tempest* IV, i, 156–57. Sunyata changed the word "on" to "of."

10. *Negative capability* refers to the ability to let go of the grasping after reasons and explanations. The term, coined by the poet John Keats (1795–1821), can be educed from this sentence in which the term was first used (taken from a letter written by Keats on December 21st, 1817):

> . . . at once it struck me what quality went to form a Man of Achievement, especially in Literature, and which Shakespeare possessed so enormously—I mean **Negative Capability**, that is, when a man is capable of being in uncertainties, mysteries, doubts, without any irritable reaching after fact and reason.

Keats meant *negative capability* to signify an ability to be free of an intellect that needs "to figure it out"; he believed that only after giving up the efforting to explain what is not explainable can there be room in the life of the mind for an intuitive awareness.

11. Sunyata recognized that "efforting" may be temporarily useful at particular stages of life, but he felt Western society had lost touch with a type of consciousness that is effort-free. He saw that only through an effort-free consciousness could one arrive at grace awareness. As he would often say, "**Effort** *was* the helper—**effort** *is* the bar."

12. This line is from stanza 4 of William Wordsworth's poem "**Elegiac Stanzas** Suggested by a Picture of Peele Castle in a Storm, Painted by Sir George Beaumont", (1807).

13. This phrase is from *King Lear V*, ii, 11:

> Men must endure
> Their going hence, even as their coming hither:
> Ripeness is all.

14. These 2 lines appear (in reverse order) in the Gnostic text called *The Gospel According to Thomas*.

15. This is often quoted as part of a longer saying:

    Effort was the helper—effort is the bar.
    Reason was the helper—reason is the bar.
    Ego was the helper—ego is the bar
    Guru was the helper—**guru** is the bar.

16. These lines are from Shakespeare's poem *The Phoenix and the Turtle* (1601).

17. This poem—called "Eternity"—was written by William Blake (1757–1827) between 1791 and 1793; it appears in his *Notebook* in a section entitled "Several Questions Answered".

18. These lines, written in 1821 by Percy Bysshe Shelley (1792–1822), are from an elegy to his dear friend John Keats; they appear in stanza 52 of the poem *Adonais*. Sunyata changed Shelley's word "Life" to "Ego-life".

19. *Hamlet* II, ii, 641.

20. These lines are from the 5th stanza of William Wordsworth's *Intimations of Immortality* (1807).

21. These lines are from the 9th stanza of the *Intimations of Immortality*.

22. *The Tempest* IV, i, 156–58. Sunyata changed the word "on" to "of."

23. These lines are from the poem *The Excursion* (1814), Book I, lines 211–16. The emphasis on " **thought was not**" was added by Sunyata.

24. From the *Notebook* written between 1791 and 1793.

25. From "Ode on a Grecian Urn" (1819), stanza 5, lines 44–45.

26. *Hamlet* II, ii, 265–66.

27. *Measure for Measure* II, ii, 117–22.

28. From the *Auguries of Innocence* (1805), lines 1–4.

29. *Nisse* is the Danish word for a household spirit—quite similar to what in English would be called a "goblin." The fairytale to which Sunyata is referring—commonly known as *The Goblin and the Grocer*—was written by Hans Christian Andersen in 1853. A new translation especially prepared for this book can be found immediately preceding these notes on page 123.

30. "Nought or all" is the battle-cry of the hero of Ibsen's play *Brand* (1866); Brand is the name of the minister who will not compromise with human weakness; he gives the speech quoted here at the conclusion of Act 4. Ibsen himself (1828–1906) was still alive when his plays were being read by Sunyata.

31. The *Imitation of Christ* (published in 1441) is attributed to the German monk Sir Thomas à Kempis (1380–1471). Both quotations are from the chapter of this work entitled "Of the Love of Solitude and Silence" (Book I, Chapter 20).

32. This is Sunyata's version of Shakespeare's line that "ripeness is all"; for the full Shakespearean quotation, see note 13.

33. Dante Alighieri, *Paradiso,* Canto XXIX, lines 70–81.

Bibliography

Anandamayi Ma. *Words of Sri Anandamayi Ma*. Translated and compiled by Atmananda. Calcutta: Shree Shree Anandamayee Charitable Society, 1982.

Arnold, Sir Edwin. *The Song Celestial*. London: Routledge & Kegan Paul, 1964. Originally published in 1885.

Brunton, Paul. *A Search in Secret India*. London: Arrow Books, 1965. Originally published in 1935. (Chapters 9, 16, and 17 describe Paul Brunton's experiences at Ramana Maharshi's ashram.)

Danielou, Alain. *The Way to the Labyrinth: Memories of East and West*. Translated from the French by Marie-Claire Cournand. New York: New Directions, 1987. (On pp. 95-96, there is a description of Dartington Hall, where Sunyata met Rabindranath Tagore; on pp. 166-168, when he tells about Sunyata, he mixes fact with fable, and falsely accuses Sunyata of stealing the possessions of the deceased local "priest.")

Dickinson, Emily. *The Complete Poems of Emily Dickinson*. Edited by Thomas H. Johnson. Boston: Little, Brown & Company, 1960.

Eliot, T.S. *Collected Poems*. New York: Harcourt Brace Jovanovich, 1970.

Huxley, Laura. *This Timeless Moment: A Personal View of Aldous Huxley*. New York: Farrar, Straus & Giroux, 1968; Rexdale, Ontario: Ambassador Books, 1968; London: Chatto & Windus, 1969. (J. Krishnamurti's description of the "religious man" is taken from the chapter entitled "Brightness".)

Ibsen, Henrik. *Brand*. This play was originally published in 1866.

Lao-tzu. *Tao Te Ching*. Translated by Stephen Mitchell. New York: Harper & Row, 1988.

Mencius. Translated with an introduction by D.C. Lau. From "The Penquin Classics" series, Penquin Books, 1970.

Merton, Thomas. *The Way of Chuang Tzu.* New York: New Directions, 1969. (These are free interpretative translations of some passages of Chuang Tzu that especially appealed to this famous Trappist monk; one of Sunyata's favorite sayings was the Merton translation of Chuang Tzu that appeared earlier in this book right after the title page.)

Nisargadatta. *I Am That: Talks with Sri Nisargadatta Maharaj.* Translated from the Maharathi tape-recordings by Maurice Frydman. Revised and edited by Sudhakar S. Dikshit. Durham, North Carolina: Acorn Press, 1984.

Nisargadatta. *Pointers from Nisargadatta Maharaj.* Adapted by Ramesh S. Balsekar. Revised and edited by Sudhakar S. Dikshit. Durham, North Carolina: Acorn Press, 1983.

The Oxford Book of English Mystical Verse. Chosen by D.H.S. Nicholson and A.H.E. Lee. London: Oxford University Press, 1924.

Patterson, Wm. Patrick. *Eating the "I": An Account of the Fourth Way—The Way of Transformation in Ordinary Life.* Edited by Barbara C. Allen. San Anselmo, California: Arete Communications, 1992. (On pp. 336-344, the author describes his meeting with Sunyata aboard the Alan Watts houseboat and his gradual realization of who Sunyata is.) Available from Arete Communications, Box 804, San Anselmo, CA 94979-0804.

Rūmī, Jalāl al-Dīn. *Night & Sleep.* Translated by Coleman Barks and Robert Bly. Cambridge, Massachusetts: Yellow Moon Press, 1981. Rūmī's poems were originally published in Persia in the thirteenth century.

Serrano, Miguel. *The Serpent of Paradise: The Story of An Indian Pilgrimage.* Translated by Frank MacShane. London: Routledge & Kegan Paul, 1974. Originally published in Great Britain by Riger & Co. in 1963. (There is a description of Serrano's meeting with Sunyata in Chapter 33; Sunyata is also "the Brother of Silence" who appears in the last words of the book.)

Serrano, Miguel. *The Visits of the Queen of Sheba*. London: Routledge & Kegan Paul, 1972. Originally published by Asia Publishing House in Bombay. (In the chapter entitled "The Brother of Silence," Sunyata is referred to as Sunya-bhai.)

Sri Wuji, Volume I (1985) and Volume II (1986). These newspaper journals contain recollections of Sunyata by those who knew him along with selections from Sunyata's own writings. Published by The Sunyata Society and available from the editors of this book at ten dollars for each volume.

Winkler, Ken. *Pilgrim of the Clear Light: The Biography of Dr. Walter Y. Evans-Wentz*. Foreword by Lama Anagarika Govinda. Berkeley, California: Dawnfire Books, 1982. Simultaneously pubished in Great Britain by Colin Smythe Ltd., Gerrards Cross, Buckinghamshire. (Sunyata is mistakenly referred to as "Norwegian by birth" on p. 66; Sunya-bhai's friendship with Dr. Evans-Wentz is mentioned in Chapter 10.)

Winkler, Ken. *A Thousand Journeys: The Biography of Lama Anagarika Govinda*. Longmead, Great Britain: Element Books, 1990. (Sunyata's companions on "Crank's Ridge" are described in the chapter on Dr. Evans-Wentz.)

Sunyata Chronology

1890 — on October 27th, he took birth with the name Alfred Julius Emmanuel Sorensen on a small farm in northern Denmark not far from Århus

1897 — enters a small country school

1898 — succumbs to a sin-complex that lingers for the next 6 years

1904 — the family farm is sold to strangers; leaves school after the 8th grade, thereby finishing his formal "headucation"; the fall into ego-consciousness that began 6 years ago is now followed by what Sunyata calls a "second innocence"

1906 — begins a 4-year apprenticeship in horticulture in Denmark

1910 — works in horticulture in Italy and France

1911 — moves to England where he works as "a simple gardener"

1913 — listens to the speeches of Annie Besant and becomes acquainted with the Theosophical movement

1929 — meets Rabindranath Tagore who casually suggests he "come to India to teach Silence"

1930 — travels to India by going overland through Palestine and Egypt and then by boat to Ceylon

1932 — makes an overland trip to England (from India) by travelling through Basrah, Babylon, Baghdad, Damascus, and Istanbul

1933 — returns to India where (except for two brief visits to Europe in the 1960's) he is to remain for the next 41 years

1935 — first hears of Ramana Maharshi from an American he meets in Kashmir—reads Paul Brunton's *A Search in Secret India* which tells the story of Brunton's meetings with Ramana Maharshi

1936 — goes to visit Ramana Maharshi and stays 2 weeks; discovers he has no questions to ask—learns from Paul Brunton that Ramana Maharshi noticed him and recognized him as a *janam-siddha* ("one of the rare-born mystics")—begins to read *The Oxford Book of English Mystical Verse.*

1937 — builds his own sanctuary-hermitage in a small cave-like hut in Karuna Kutir near Almora (in the foothills of the Indian Himalayas); Lama Anagarika Govinda and Dr. W.Y. Evans-Wentz are his neighbors

1938 — visits Ramana Maharshi for the second time

1940 — on his 3rd visit, Ramana Maharshi telepathically transmits these five English words:

We are always aware sunyata.

Emmanuel Sorensen takes this message as recognition, initiation, mantra, and name.

1945 — writes reflections that he calls **Memory**

1946 — makes his 4th and last visit to see Ramana Maharshi

1953 — becomes a citizen of India

1964 — visits family and friends in Europe after being away more than 3 decades

1974 — makes his visit to California as a guest of the Alan Watts Society; he is told that if he comes to live in California, it is with the promise that "reality-wise, Sunyata need not **do** anything"

1975 — returns to India, but begins making preparation to leave his hermitage in the Himalayas and move to California

1978 — comes to live in Mill Valley, California; while making yearly forays to Chicago, he is to remain in the United States for the last 6 years of his life

1980 — writes a new "beginning" to replace the missing pages of **Memory**

1984 — on Sunday, August 5th, he is struck by a car while crossing a street in Fairfax, California; that evening his body lapses into a coma—on Monday, August 13th, he "comes home"

Glossary

akasha — the most subtle of the five elements, the ether; the all-pervading space around us

ambrosia — the food of the gods that grants immortality to those mortals who eat it (in Greek and Roman mythology)

amrit — the nectar of the gods that grants immortality to those mortals who drink it (in Hindu mythology)

ananda — grace

anandaful — full of grace; more than mere happiness

ashram — the spiritual community that grows up around a *guru*; a place where the Self is honored

atman — the Self; the seed of perfection in all beings

avatar — an embodied form of God who comes to earth for the purpose of restoring the moral order

aware (used as a verb as in *to aware*) — the act of becoming aware

bhagavan (occasionally *bhagawan* or *bhagwan*) — literally, this means 'the Lord' or 'God'; it is used as a term of reverence when addressing one who is Self-realized

bhai — friend (in Hindi)

bodhisattva — one who has returned to the wheel of birth and death for the benefit of all sentient beings

Brahman — the Absolute, the impersonal Supreme Reality; it is unchanging and eternal

chela — disciple (in Hindi)

darshan — literally, "looking at" the spiritual teacher; an audience with a saint, sage, or diety; this brings the blessing of his or her being; the devotee "has" *darshan*, the guru "gives" it

dharma — the natural law of the cosmic order; conduct in life that is right and true; a course of action that is decreed for each individual which will best foster that individual's spiritual growth while simultaneously enabling that individual to fulfill her or his societal duties and obligations

diksha — initiation; bestowed by the look, word, or touch of the *guru*, it is a gift of the Self to the Self

egoji(es) — a term of endearment used by Sunyata to refer to egos; in India the suffix "ji" put at the end of any term indicates both respect and affection

Emmanuel — in Hebrew, it means "God with us"; as this is the name given to the Messiah prophesied in the Old Testament (*Isaiah* 7:14), Jesus is called Emmanuel in the New Testament (*Matthew* 1:23); it was one of the names that Sunyata's mother chose for him and his own favorite Western name for himself

guru — a spiritual guide and teacher who has realized the Self; as it is derived from the Sanskrit roots *gu* (darkness) and *ru* (dispelled), it literally means "the one who dispels darkness"

headucation — mental conditioning; while "education" draws out that which is within, "headucation" focuses attention on that which is without

innerstances — what happens within; it is akin to "circumstances," but refers only to inward events

innerstanding — a way of comprehending that requires no words, thought, or even effort; it is akin to "understanding," but is not mental

janam-siddha — a rare-born mystic; one who is perfected (*siddha*) at birth (*janam*)

ji ji muge — perfect, unimpeded, mutual interpenetration; from the Japanese words *ji* (thing) and *muge* (interdiffusion)

jnana — wisdom; the realization that comes when all events, things, and beings are seen as manifestations of the Self

jnani — one who perceives God continuously and effortlessly in all events, things, and beings; it is a synonym for the Self since there is no longer any ego to perceive the Self after Self-realization

Jutes — the Danish people (in Danish)

Jutland — the peninsula of Northern Europe that forms the mainland of Denmark (in Danish)

karma — action, the result of action, as well as the law of cause and effect by which a person reaps what is sown; *karma* originates when the individual self in her or his ignorance functions as an active agent; when a person realizes her or his true nature, she or he no longer continues to create *karma*

lila — life's play; the divine play of the Self

lingam — a symbol of the unmanifest Shiva in the shape of a vertical cylinder with a rounded top

memory — an awareness of living harmonies, wholeness, and unity that precedes ego-consciousness; a natural pre-natal light of awareness

negative capability — the ability to remain in uncertainty, mystery, and doubt without any need to grasp for either facts or explanations; it is a quality of mind that enhances intuition

Nisse — goblin (in Danish)

perfectum est — perfection is (in Latin); the view that from the highest perspective everything is perfect

prarabdha — fixed, unchangeable *karma* that must be experienced during one's lifetime; destiny *purnam* — perfect, whole, complete; that which is not limited by time or space

Sadguru — the *guru* who is Real and True

sadhana — the way one comes to Truth; spiritual practice for the purpose of preparing oneself for Self-realization

samata — unchanging centeredness in equanamity; sameness of mood regardless of circumstances

samsara — the wheel of birth and death; the cycle of life in the world through an ongoing series of generations and extinctions; except for the *bodhisattva*, birth is a result of ignorance of the true nature of the Self

sat-chit-ananda — although this is commonly translated as 'existence—knowledge—bliss', Sunyata felt its true meaning was closer to **'being—awareness—grace'**

satsang — the meetings of people on a spiritual path; association (*sanga*) with truth (*sat*)

Self — the infinite God-energy immanent in all creation

Shakti — the active power of God; the energy that makes the world run

shakti-antics — efforting that pretends to be Spiritual

shakti-business — a way of being busy in the world wherein one loses contact with the spiritual dimension

Shiva-eye — the third eye; it is located in the center of the forehead between the two eyes; the place from where the Truth is directly perceived

siddhi — a super-normal faculty; the power to perform "miracles"

soma juice — a drink offered to the gods and then drunk by mortals in order to induce a divine mood

sunyata — full solid emptiness; the Void; the Buddhist doctrine that all beings and phenomena are free of any soul or intrinsic nature — the no-body-ness of all beings and the no-thing-ness of all phenomena

Swa-lila — Self-play; the God that plays in all of this; there is nothing but God

Swa-raj — Self-rule; the Self governing the Self

tantric — a path that allows the expression of desires so that eventually they can be transcended

Tao — the Way, the course of Nature, the flow of things, the pathless path (in Chinese)

Tat — That; the impersonal Supreme Reality

Tat twam asi — literally, 'That thou art', it is usually translated as **'thou art That'**; this is a common Indian expression signifying that each seemingly separate being is none other than the Self

Wu! — both "yes" and "no" simultaneously

Wuji — refers to Sunyata's higher Self; it was also the name given to his pet dog Wuti after Wuti died and entered into the Invisible Real

yoga — literally, "union"; the way through which an individual attains union with the Self

Biographical Sketches

Betty Camhi worked as a private and public school teacher in the field of special education in the San Francisco Bay area. She has a degree in Psychology from the City College of New York and has worked extensively with children who are considered to have learning disabilities. She was involved in Sufism prior to serving as Sunyata's secretary and chauffeur. She currently resides in Medford, Oregon.

Elliott Isenberg is a psychologist in private practice in San Francisco. Starting in 1966, he lived and travelled in Europe, Africa, and Asia for seven years. In March of 1973, he met his guru Neem Karoli Baba in Vrindavan, India. He studied at Amherst College and the London School of Economics before completing a doctorate in Psychology at the California Institute of Integral Studies.